Legal Liability and
Risk Management in
Adventure Tourism

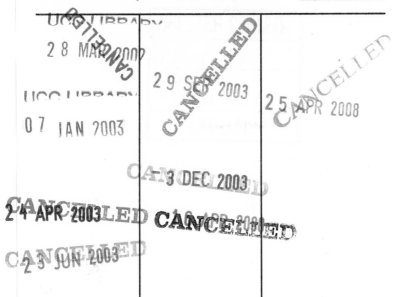

ROSS CLOUTIER

with Daniel Garvey, Will Leverette,
James Moss & Gilles Valade

WARNING
This book is not intended to provide legal advice to its readers. It makes every attempt to be accurate but recognizes that laws change and that they vary between different legal jurisdictions. Before relying on any of the information in this book , you should consult with your attorney and abide by his or her advice. We take no responsibility for any reliance on the information contained in this text.

Legal Liability and Risk Management in Adventure Tourism
by Ross Cloutier
with Daniel Garvey, Will Leverette, James Moss, Gilles Valade

Copyright 2000
Bhudak Consultants Ltd.
#171, 230 – 1210 Summit Drive
Kamloops, British Columbia V2C 6M1

Cover photograph: Magnus Image Bank
Interior photographs courtesy: John Clarke, Pat Morrow, Geoff Powter, Jim Martinello,
                              Steve Ludwig, Roger Laurilla, Roger Chayer

Copy editing: Anne Ryall
Layout and design: digital banff graphic arts
Printed in Canada by Hignell Printing, Winnipeg

Canadian Cataloguing in Publication Data

Cloutier, K. Ross, 1956–
   Legal liability and risk management in adventure tourism
Includes bibliographical references and index.
   ISBN 0–9682474–1–5

1. Liability (Law) — Canada. 2. Tourist trade — Law and legislation — Canada.
3. Risk Management
I. Garvey, Daniel II. Title
KE1232.Z85C56 2000   346.7103'1   C00-911134-4
KF1250.A2C56 2000

Introduction

The adventure industry is a unique entity. It comprises a wide variety of commercial and recreational interests that combine to form a diversified and sometimes disparate field. Its history in Canada is relatively short, resulting in relatively few litigation cases from which to draw direct rulings. Consequently, there is a wide variance and incongruity of knowledge among programmers, instructors, guides and business operators across the country regarding which laws are relevant, how the courts would rule on a particular situation and how specific standard operating procedures would measure up. It is important that a consistent base of information about legal liability be dispersed throughout the industry, as exposure to liability is considered by most operators to be inherent in their activities.

A second element in the equation is the practice of risk management. The knowledge and practice of risk management within the adventure industry has become very sophisticated; helicopters full of skiers crash without the incident making the newspapers, and legal contracts accepting negligent actions on the part of operators are signed regularly by clients. Once again, however, the new, isolated or smaller operator does not always understand the strategies used by the sophisticated operation. Adventure has become big business — with substantial risks, returns and rewards. The management of risk is a daily concern for operators, who need to protect clients, guides and business value.

This book has been written as an attempt to compile much of the knowledge base concerning legal liability and risk management as they are known and practised throughout the adventure industry. The two topics are very different but integrally related, and this text attempts to link them in a manner that can be clearly understood by the lay reader. The book starts with a selection of legal concepts and related discussions about how these concepts apply to adventure activities. A background on risk management is then presented, followed by a demonstration of how risk management is applied to adventure activities. It is impossible to write a text that applies to all legal jurisdictions or that contains every legal concept. What we have attempted to accomplish here is to raise points that have similarities in a wide variety of jurisdictions.

The practice of adventure used to be carried out by alternate-lifestyle activists. These days, it has become commercialized and enough of an economic driver that it draws worldwide attention. Exposure to liability, and the need to practise risk management are realities inherent in the activities of adventure businesses. Adventure operators need to understand the various elements of these realities and the interactions between them in order to provide professional programs that are as safe as possible for their participants and for the adventure companies themselves.

Acknowledgements

This publication has been a huge project spread out over many years of research and information gathering. Thanks are owed to the authors who contributed sections of the book: Daniel Garvey, Will Leverette, James Moss and Gilles Valade. Thanks are also due to my lawyer friends, Don Blakely and Keith Parkhari, who proofread the text and made many valuable comments.

Special thanks are owed to Anne Ryall, who edited the text, and Geoff Powter, who did the layout. Without them I'd be lost.

Contents

Chapter Seven ✧ Canadian Businesses Carrying out Operations in the United States — by James Moss

Chapter Eight ✧ Risk Management

Chapter Nine ✧ Preparing Risk-management Documents

Chapter Ten ❖ Guidelines for Handling an Accident

Chapter Eleven ❖ An International Perspective — by Daniel Garvey

Chapter Twelve ❖ Risk Management and Guides

Chapter Thirteen ❖ Insurance — by Gilles Valade

Chapter One

The Legal System in Canada

Common Law

Canada's legal system evolved from the legal systems of England and France. After the 12th century in England, the courts started becoming more centralized and the King's court began to keep records. By the 16th century, these records had created enough of a foundation of cases that they had become useful as a source of common rulings. The development of a significant trend in rulings over the following years produced what became known as the *common law* of England. The settlement of English colonies in North America brought the common law of England across the Atlantic.

The Treaty of Paris (1763), which resulted from the English capture of the French colonies during the Seven Years War, applied English law in what was then New France. The *Quebec Act* (1774) required Quebec to follow English law in criminal matters but allowed it to continue to follow the Customs of Paris in civil matters. In 1866, the new *Quebec Civil Code* was adopted.

Although both Canada and the United States share the same English heritage, the War of Independence changed much for the United States through the severing of its political and legal ties with England. Nonetheless, many American states at the time of the war adopted English common law — with local modifications. After the war, the United States developed a dual court system comprising state and federal courts, while new states brought additional legal history with them.

The common law is sometimes referred to as *case law* because it is found not in a code but in the recorded judgements of courts. It operates on the rule of precedent, or *stare decisis*, which requires that "like cases be decided alike". This means that a court must decide a case based on the judgement of previous, similar cases. The common law is therefore different from statutes, which are written laws established by governments through legislation.

It takes a long period of time for clear and concise common law to become established, as it must first absorb many customs, legal principles and social values. Common law is intended to be equitable — fair to the parties based on principles and rules even in situations where the law might not apply directly. It is also intended to continuously evolve, accounting for society's current norms and values.

Statute Law

Laws passed by federal or provincial legislatures are called *statutes*, or *acts*. A statute passes through a process consisting of a proposal, two readings, a clause-by-clause review by a legislative committee, a third reading, and an assent by the Lieutenant-Governor (provincial) or Governor-General (federal) before being proclaimed as law. The body that originally passed a statute may amend it. Statutes may be used to make new laws or to codify a common law. Regulations are developed to add specifics to legislation and are part of the statutory structure.

As mentioned earlier, the province of Quebec has codified much of its common law in what is known as the *Quebec Civil Code*.

Law and the Adventure Industry

Organizations and businesses that carry out adventure-activity programming are susceptible to both common and statute laws. For example, common-law judgements surrounding the use of legal-release contracts between an adventure organization and its clients have established norms for their content requirements and the process of their delivery. Relevant statute laws applicable to adventure programs include such acts as the *Motor Vehicle Act*, the *Workers' Compensation Act* and a variety of travel and tourism acts, among others.

The Court System

In Canada, a number of different courts can rule on a civil case (a case that is not a criminal matter). Although each province's court structure is unique, the courts tend to divide into three levels. At the first level are those courts that deal with less serious family, civil and criminal matters. The second level consists of the superior courts, which deal with major civil and criminal matters and act as appeal courts for the lower courts. The third level is composed of the courts of appeal, which hear appeals from the provincial superior courts.

At the federal level, the Federal Court of Canada hears claims against the federal government. The Supreme Court of Canada is the highest appeal court in the country and may hear appeals from any provincial or federal court.

Civil Court Procedure

Before civil cases proceed to trial, the plaintiff and the defendant exchange a number of documents called *pleadings*. Usually the plaintiff will file a *writ of summons* against the plaintiff which describes the wrongs committed by the defendant to the plaintiff. Once having received the writ, the defendant files a document called an *appearance*, which states that he or she will defend the case.

The plaintiff then files a statement of claim with the court and the defendant which provides the details and facts of the claim. At this point the defendant prepares a statement of defense which presents his or her point of view in relation to the facts and describes how the case will be defended.

The two parties may exchange requests for further information or file an amended statement of claim or defense. They may then hold an *examination for discovery*, where questions under oath between both parties are transcribed. These transcripts may be used later at the trial.

Often parties will attempt to settle their dispute prior to going to trial. In fact, the majority of cases are settled before trial after the discovery process has taken place.

If a trial is initiated, the plaintiff's lawyer begins by stating the issues and facts that he or she is going to attempt to prove. The plaintiff's side calls witnesses, and evidence is given. The defendant's lawyer may cross-examine the witnesses called by the plaintiff.

Once the plaintiff's case has been presented, the defendant may ask the judge to dismiss the case because the evidence has not proved the plaintiff's claim. The judge may rule the case to continue, and the defendant must call witnesses and attempt to prove that the claim is untrue. The plaintiff's lawyer may cross-examine the defendant's witnesses.

Once both sides have presented their cases, each side may summarize its case and present its interpretation of the law to the judge. The judge will then give his or her judgement and provide rationale for it in writing. If the plaintiff wins the case, the judge may order the defendant to pay the plaintiff's costs of defending the case. Alternatively, if the defendant wins the case, the judge may order the plaintiff to pay the defendant the costs of defending the case:

> To say that one side may be told to pay the "costs" of the other does not necessarily mean a full reimbursement of legal expenses. Such costs are typically paid out according to a pre-determined scale and only rarely will the costs paid cover the total legal expenses. In fact, in frivolous cases a plaintiff may decide not to sue because they know they will not get reimbursement of full legal costs even if they win and their legal costs may exceed any potential settlement. (1)

If either side thinks that the judge has erred in his or her decision, it may file a notice of appeal to the relevant appeal court. The appeal court may admit the appeal and reverse the decision, may change the decision, may send the case back for a new trial or may affirm the judgement and dismiss the appeal.

Every common-law decision handed down by a judge is based on previously ruled cases and statutes. The new decision needs to be consistent with previous law and will then become part of common-law principles.

Notes to Chapter One

1. Don Blakely (Attorney at Law), communication, February 21, 2000.

Chapter Two

Tort Law

Introduction

The law of torts hovers over virtually every activity undertaken by an adventure organization. The driver of the company van, the instructor of the adventure-sport activity, the guide who provides advice to a client, and the manufacturer of equipment must each abide by the standards of tort law. It is likely that all workers involved in any stage of providing an adventure product have at least a superficial awareness of the need to exercise care in what they do — and of the potential for lawsuit even when they do exercise reasonable care.

The term *tort* is derived from the Latin word *tortus*, meaning "crooked" or "twisted", and has evolved in English to mean "wrong". Although a variety of definitions exist, the most useful for our purposes is "A tort is a civil wrong, other than a breach of contract, which the law will redress by an award of damages." (1) In other words, the courts will decide whether to order a defendant to pay compensation to a plaintiff for a wrong the defendant did to the plaintiff. The wrong need not be intentional; indeed, adventure businesses on the whole try to prevent wrongs through appropriate risk-management techniques. But accidents will happen despite even the most rigorous prevention techniques, and tort law says that they may require compensation; the court will decide if so, and how much.

Tort wrongs generally fall into two broad categories: intentional interference and unintentional interference. Intentional interference tends to refer to such wrongs as assault and battery, false imprisonment, defamation, libel, slander, trespass, willful damage, deceit and fraud. Unintentional interference refers to such wrongs as negligence, nuisance and manufacturers' liability. Most adventure lawsuits revolve around unintentional acts such as negligence, and it is these types of issues which will be the focus of this chapter.

Fault-based Accident Compensation

Tort law is primarily concerned with compensation for "fault-based" accidents, where injuries to one person have been caused by the fault of another and this can be proved based on the facts of the case. Courts rule on who is at fault in order to compensate victims, punish wrongdoers and deter future wrongdoing by others. "Compensation" means to put the victim back into the position he or she would have been in were it not for the wrong.

An important by-product of these common-law rulings is that they clarify the appropriate standard of care, make statements as to appropriate societal values and keep the market in check by making it bear the full cost of its mishaps without the addition of written statutes to keep it in line.

Negligence

Negligence cases dominate adventure-industry lawsuits in their frequency and importance. Did the guide give inappropriate advice? Did the client contribute to his or her own accident?

Did the instructor use appropriate equipment? Was the equipment in suitable condition? Was there a reasonable standard of care provided? These are all negligence issues faced by the adventure operator every day.

The classic definition of *negligence* is "the omission to do something which a reasonable man, guided upon those considerations which ordinarily regulate the conduct of human affairs, would do, or doing something which a prudent and reasonable man would not do". (2) Negligence refers to conduct that falls below the standard required — in this case, of the adventure industry — by the industry itself and by the society in which it functions.

Elements of a Negligent Action

In order to establish negligence, five elements must be proved:

- ✧ There must be injury to the plaintiff.
- ✧ The defendant must have had a duty to avoid injuring the plaintiff.
- ✧ The defendant's conduct must have breached the standard of care required by law.
- ✧ The conduct of the defendant must be a proximate cause of the damage.
- ✧ There should be no factors in the plaintiff's conduct which justify a reduction or an elimination of the damages awarded, such as being guilty of contributory negligence or voluntarily assuming the legal risk.

Duty of Care

In order for a defendant to be held responsible for an injury to a plaintiff, the defendant must be held to have had a duty of care to the plaintiff. *Duty of care* in negligence law refers to the responsibility of one party to take reasonable care for the protection of another party. It is based on "the neighbour principle", which states that one "must take reasonable care to avoid acts or omissions which [one] can reasonably foresee would be likely to injure [one's] neighbor". (3) Only where a duty of care is said to exist can a breach be proved.

The definition of duty of care introduces the concept of *reasonable foreseeability*, which is critical in determining negligence. Reasonable foreseeability is based on a mythical person — the reasonable person — and is used in determining both a duty and, later on, a standard of care. In the adventure industry, it is generally accepted that the commercial relationship between guide and client creates a responsibility for the guide to care for the client. However, the question is commonly raised: Does the guide have a duty of care to non-clientele whom he or she may meet in the field?

The law of negligence does not recognize a duty of care to all individuals; rather, it recognizes a duty of care only to reasonably foreseeable victims. This may include clients, as well as others for whom a guide assumes responsibility. The plaintiff must have been foreseeable as a victim in order for the defendant to be liable. It is reasonably foreseeable that careless guiding puts at risk clients, other guides and volunteers — which is why these people are owed a duty of care. It is also reasonably foreseeable that guides could injure third parties in the vicinity such as other recreationists who are not clients. In addition, one client may be held responsible for injury to another client. (4)

However, where the defendant accidentally injures an "unforeseeable victim", he or she will not be held liable for that person's injuries. An example of such a situation would be where the guide did not realize that the victim was in the area or where the victim was so far removed from the guide's activities that the injury could not be reasonably foreseen.

When There Is a Duty to Others

Many relationships impose a duty to assist others or to prevent them from being injured. These include such situations as where there is an economic relationship between the two parties, where one party supervises or controls the other, where one party has created the dangerous situation, where one party voluntarily assumes responsibility for the other and where one party is the occupier of land or premises.

The fact that the relationship is economic, and not gratuitous, is important. The Supreme Court of Canada ruled on the economic relationship after an intoxicated competitor suffered injuries during a tubing race: "[W]hen a ski resort establishes a competition in a highly dangerous sport and runs the competition for profit, it owes a duty of care towards visibly intoxicated persons." (5) In another case, the Supreme Court ruled that the economic association involved in doing business is that of an "invitor-invitee" relationship and that a higher duty of care exists in this situation than for persons in general. (6)

Persons who enter relationships where they are expected to control or supervise do so knowing that they are responsible for protecting others from being injured and that they may need to assist those in their care if they fall into danger. Parents and daycare centres are responsible for protecting the children in their care, (7) teachers must protect their students from harm, (8) informal employers have a duty to protect their friends when these friends act as informal employees, (9) the master of a boat has a duty to assist a passenger who falls overboard, (10) and the owner of a motorcycle has a duty to protect anybody he or she lends it to from harm. (11)

Where a person who is initially under no obligation to assist another person begins to assist, through his or her words or conduct, a duty to continue to assist develops. (12) By beginning to assist, one may be creating a dependence on that assistance by preventing assistance from others. On the other hand, where an individual who is under no legal obligation to assist neither prevents other help from being offered nor worsens the victim's condition by beginning to assist, liability will not be imposed. (13) This may be modified somewhat by "Good Samaritan" legislation in various jurisdictions.

Occupier liability requires an occupier to maintain premises and activities on those premises which are reasonably safe. An occupier's duty of care extends to all natural or man-made hazards and to the removal or mitigation of any such hazards. (14)

When There Is No Duty to Others

Although professional codes of ethics may require a professional to render assistance to another person in danger, the law does not. The legal issue is whether the law of torts should require a bystander who has not been a party to the creation of a dangerous situation or who has not voluntarily assumed responsibility for that person, to act to assist the person in danger. "Assisting" may refer to helping someone who is in danger, someone who is injured or someone who could be warned to avoid harm.

This is the dilemma described by Jesus in Luke, Chapter 10, when he tells the story of the priest, the Levite and the Samaritan. The priest and the Levite pass by a man who has been robbed and beaten. The Samaritan stops, provides "first aid", transports the injured person to an inn and pays for the man's care and lodging until he is better. As stated in one case: "[T]he priest and Levite who passed on the other side were not, it is supposed, liable at law for the continued suffering of the man who fell among the thieves, which they might, and morally ought to have, prevented or relieved." (15) Similarly: "[N]o principle is more deeply rooted in the common law than that there is no duty to take positive action in aid of another no matter how helpless or perilous his position is," (16) and: "[I]t appears presently in the law that one can, with immunity, smoke a cigarette on the beach while one's neighbor drowns and, without a word of warning, watch a child or blind person walk into certain danger." (17)

While the two situations in the last quote are extreme and hardly imaginable, it appears that the law imposes no duty to "render assistance to those in peril, in the absence of a special relationship, even where assistance can be rendered easily, and without risk or inconvenience to the rescuer". (18) The rationale for this position is that Canadian tort law is a corrective system that requires those individuals who injure others to compensate the injured for their loss; it is not a moral persuader and does not require individuals to rescue others. Though it could, the law does not view this as a criminal matter — contrary to the common European approach.

The presence of a duty to rescue depends on whether the observer voluntarily assumed responsibility for the person in danger, as in the situation where a guide assumes responsibility for non-clients while in the field. However, care must be taken: "Those who attempt in good faith to assist someone in peril expose themselves to potential civil liability if they bungle the attempt, but those who stand idly by without lifting a finger incur no liability, although the latter conduct is probably more reprehensible and more deserving of a civil sanction." (19) These are muddy waters, as it is possible to mismanage a rescue attempt and not worsen the position of the already-injured person and it is also possible to be careful and yet worsen the position of the injured party.

In addition, there may well be a duty to rescue when the guide (or any other individual) has been a party to the creation of the situation. The responsibility here is obvious; as one of the causes of the danger, the guide has an obligation to make it right.

Standard of Care

Negligence law finds a defendant liable based not solely on whether he or she had a duty to care for a plaintiff but also on whether the defendant met a reasonable standard of care. The standard required is determined by considering the specific things that should or should not have been done in caring for the plaintiff. By examining the facts placed before the court, the judge or jury decides in essence to what standard the duty of care should have been carried out. This is usually the standard of the "reasonable person".

The Reasonable Person

The standard of the "reasonable person" measures the negligent person against another, hypothetical person who is in the same situation. A reasonable person is expected to be of normal intelligence and to apply reasonable care towards others. (20) Said another way:

> Negligence is the omission to do something which a reasonable man, guided upon those considerations which ordinarily regulate the conduct of human affairs, would do, or doing something which a prudent and reasonable man would not do. (21)

The law requires a minimum level of performance, whether the person is capable of it or not, and pleading that one did "the best [one] knew how" (22) is not an adequate defense. The defendant is held to carry out the same standard of care as that which would be expected of a reasonable and careful person carrying out the same activity. He or she is not "a person of infinite resources" (23) and is not obligated to "exercise the best possible judgement in an emergency" (24) or to "avoid all risks". (25)

We can conclude from the above comments that the reasonable adventure guide or instructor is one who acts prudently, exercises ordinary intelligence and decision making, is not required to display the highest skill possible and does not possess unusual foresight. A defendant guide or instructor will be evaluated against the actions and decisions that a reasonable guide or instructor would make in his or her place, and negligence will be proved only when the defendant's conduct falls below the standard expected of a reasonable guide carrying out the same activity. However: "[S]ome persons are by nature unduly timorous and imagine every path beset with lions. Others, of more robust temperament, fail to foresee or nonchalantly disregard even the most obvious dangers. The reasonable man is presumed to be free both from over-apprehension and from over-confidence." (26)

Expert Knowledge and the Standard of Care

Guides and instructors of adventure activities present themselves as having expert knowledge. As with other professions, the courts will therefore have higher expectations of these individuals. The higher expectations are based on the assumption of responsibility for others more than on the fact that the relationship may be an economic or contractual one. (27) "Even if one is not an expert, if there [is] representation that one is such, and if that representation is relied upon by the plaintiff, it can result in one being held to an expert's level of standard of care." (28)

The care required of a professional person is that degree of care that is shown by the reasonably prudent practitioner operating in like circumstances. (29) It therefore becomes crucial to understand the established professional customs and general practices in the relevant field:

> It is an error of law for a judge to hold a professional liable for negligence where it has been shown that there is a body of competent, professional opinion that supports the conduct of the defendant. Where there is evidence of generally approved practice, according to qualified and skilled professionals, compliance with this practice must be regarded as reasonable. (30)

It follows that it is important for a guide to be absolutely certain that he or she is familiar with professional customs and norms. This highlights the need to be able to demonstrate adequate training and ongoing professional development.

Generally, what constitutes "custom and generally approved practice" will be determined by expert witnesses: "Except in those unusual ... negligence cases where the standard of care is a matter of common knowledge, the jury must determine the standard of professional learning, skill and care required of a defendant ... only from the opinions of ... expert witnesses (including the defendant witness) as to such standard." (31) However, as there is often no consensus as to approved practice and the issue at hand may not be entirely technical in nature, the issue may be one that can be judged by the non-professional person and the court may not treat the professional practice as conclusive: (32)

> I accept the evidence of approved practice is most helpful and persuasive and I fully recognize an absence of expertise in [medical] matters on the part of the Court. In my view, however, a court has a right to strike down substandard approved practice when common sense dictates such a result. (33)

The courts are clear that individuals are expected to gain sufficient knowledge and experience prior to undertaking an activity: "Where individuals engage in activities for which they lack sufficient knowledge or experience, they will be at fault, not so much for their inability to carry out the activity, but for their decision to attempt the activity without accounting for their deficiencies." (34) A guide needs to be able to prove the existence of this knowledge in court. The more formal the training and certification demonstrated, the better off the guide will be.

Standard of Care of Specialists
The courts may hold a specialist to a higher standard of care than a generalist. The law is clear in this regard in both the medical (35) and the legal (36) professions, and the principles apply elsewhere: "If the client engages an expert, and ...expects to pay commensurate fees, is he not entitled to expect ...more than the standard of the reasonably competent?" (37)

Clients rightfully expect more from specialists than from general practitioners; however: "the court may find that although the general practitioner may not be required to live up to the same level of competence as a specialist, they will be negligent for undertaking work in circumstances where the reasonable general practitioner would have sought the assistance of specialists." (38)

The same applies to practitioners starting in their fields: "Negligence law requires beginners to appreciate their own limitations, and seek specialist help or referrals, and requires their supervisors to take into account the inexperience of these beginners." (39)

Disclosure

When making decisions for clients regarding routes and hazards, a professional guide is faced with the question of how much information to disclose to a client regarding the risks associated with the different choices available. The closest relevant standard of care I have found is that of the medical profession (although there are many similar rulings concerning lawyers), and analogies may be drawn from this information when making guiding decisions.

The law regarding the responsibility of a doctor to inform the patient about the nature, gravity and risks involved with medical treatment, and the patient's right to make an informed choice concerning which treatment will be performed has been expanded to encompass much wider disclosure. (40) The patient has the right to be fully informed of all "risks of treatment". (41) This is termed "informed consent" and is "not unlike the duty of a manufacturer to warn about the dangerous properties of their products". (42)

A doctor's duty to inform relates to all the material, special or unusual risks of treatment. (43) What is material is determined by what the reasonable patient would like to know, and not by what the reasonable doctor would like to disclose, (44) and the duty to inform is more onerous if the patient asks more specific questions or if the doctor knows in some way that the patient would like a fuller explanation. (45)

A first reaction to the widely encompassing concepts that apply to the medical profession might leave the adventure guide or instructor with a heightened concern regarding his or her duty to disclose the risks that are part of the profession. It must be remembered, however, that the plaintiff would have to prove that damages were caused by a breach in this duty, i.e. that, had the required information been communicated, the client would have declined to participate. This would be difficult, but not impossible, to achieve.

The courts do not require doctors to explain to their patients all the details of every procedure and all the things that can possibly go wrong. If that were the case, our doctors would be discussing medicine all day rather than practicing it. The courts do not want doctors to confuse or frighten their patients or to burden them with unnecessary data. There is no need to tell a patient about the ordinary risks ... since everyone is expected to know about them. Thus, just as one need not warn that a match will burn or that a knife will cut, because that would be redundant, a doctor need not disclose that, if an incision is made, there will normally be some bleeding, some pain and a scar will remain when the cut has healed. (46)

In deciding a case, the court will determine whether the information given to the patient (or guided client) in the circumstances was sufficient. This may be a new concept for much of the adventure industry to apply, as often an authoritative guiding style is used that sets the guide up to make all route-finding and hazard-assessment decisions — rather than an approach that educates clients about the options available and has them accept the risks associated with one of those options. However, if a defense is to be based on the voluntary assumption of risk, where it is claimed that the client clearly knew of and assumed the risks inherent in the activity, then the client must clearly be made aware of the risks and options — and be part of the decision-making process.

For example: What of a guide who has the choice of three potential routes — all with varying levels of risk — and who chooses not to take clients on the route with the least risk? An accident occurs, and the client argues in court that the levels of risk were not clearly communicated and that, if they had been, the client would have wanted to be taken on the route with the least amount of risk.

Further complicating this issue in Canada is that a defense based on assumption of risk is not possible without an express agreement (*see Chapter Six*).

Causation

The third element in a negligence action is that the defendant's behaviour must be connected to the plaintiff's injury. Negligent defendants are not liable unless their conduct is a *proximate cause* of the plaintiff's losses. This cannot be overstated: in negligence law, the defendant must have caused the injury suffered by the plaintiff, and the injury must not be too *remote*. This is the foundation of *fault-based* compensation.

There are two relevant principles at work within the concept of causation. The first is that of *cause-in-fact*, i.e. establishing whether the defendant's action was the basis of the injury. The second principle is that of *remoteness*, i.e. determining the extent of the defendant's liability.

For example: Will an adventure company that operates a backcountry lodge be held liable for damages to guided clients in an avalanche accident? What if the victims were non-guided clients skiing by themselves? What if the plaintiffs were not paying clients but were skiing lodge-controlled runs? What if a guide gave route advice to recreational skiers who entered the lodge's permit area? What if recreational skiers followed a guided party's uptrack across an avalanche-prone slope and were buried — even though the guide may have warned them not to follow?

It can be seen that many factors affect the "connection" between the parties and thus the level of responsibility involved.

Cause-in-fact

In order for the defendant to be liable to the plaintiff, negligence law requires that the defendant's misconduct be connected to the plaintiff's injury. There must be a reason to hold the defendant liable. No single method exists for determining this, and the courts are flexible in how they approach the issue.

One approach used by the courts is to establish whether it can be proved that the plaintiff's injuries would not have occurred "but for" the defendant's negligent conduct. In order to do this, the court must determine what would have occurred without the defendant's conduct, which is difficult to ascertain.

There is nothing to say that the defendant's actions need be the entire cause of the event. Often, numerous factors come together to create an event, and the plaintiff's actions may be a "material contribution" to the injury. Presumably, apportionment laws would then allow a defendant to be held liable for a percentage of the injury and to pay damages accordingly:

> It is not, in my view, incumbent upon the plaintiff in a case such as this to prove positively that the presence of the crash mat would have prevented the injury. The plaintiff is bound to prove, according to a balance of probabilities, that the failure of the school authorities to provide more adequate matting and insist upon its use contributed to the accident. (47)

Where additional causes combine to create an injury or combine to create a greater injury than would otherwise have happened, the plaintiff may have separate claims on each action. This may be a case where multiple defendants are jointly responsible for the injuries or where the same defendant causes multiple actions.

In a case involving multiple defendants, additional causes may occur simultaneously or successively. Where the causes occur simultaneously, all defendants will be held jointly liable for the plaintiff's injury. (48) Where they occur successively, the courts generally adopt one of three different approaches:

> The first approach is to treat both actors as jointly responsible for the plaintiff's loss, as would be done if the acts occurred simultaneously. The second has been to argue that the second tort has overtaken the first, so that the first tortfeasor is responsible only for the plaintiff's loss up to the time of the second tort, and the second tortfeasor is responsible for the loss thereafter. The third approach has been to hold the first tortfeasor liable for all of the plaintiff's losses, which resulted from the first tort, and to hold the second tortfeasor liable only for whatever additional losses may have flowed from the second. Canadian courts have favored the third approach.... Courts assess the losses from the first tort as if the action for this tort had been tried immediately before the second tort occurred. (49)

Remoteness

Remoteness deals with the extent of a defendant's legal responsibility and financial liability for injuries caused to a plaintiff. (50) The courts have a strong tendency to hold a business liable for a client's injury, though this may hold true only to a certain point and may depend on the foreseeability of the accident. (51) Once having determined that the defendant had a duty, breached that duty and was the cause of the plaintiff's injury, the court must determine the extent of the defendant's liability.

Remoteness tends to be one of the most difficult aspects of a negligence case, and the application of this concept has varied in its broadness over time. Generally speaking, courts have struggled with the issue of remoteness and today tend to hold defendants responsible for a wider range of activities than in the past. This is largely because the court may feel the need to find someone to pay the costs of the injury, and the business is the most able. Imagine the paraplegic child and his or her subsequent care costs and the onerous responsibility these costs would impose on most families.

Although there is no automatic formula for determining how remote a defendant's actions need to be before he or she will not be held liable, the tendency is to assume the worst. For a perspective on current thought, consider the following quotes from one of the leading commentators in this field:

> It would also be helpful if the courts would approach these remoteness cases with the attitude that a person found to have been negligent should only be relieved of liability if the result of the negligence was truly "freakish", "one in a million", "fantastic or improbable." In other words, there should be an assumption of liability unless the court is convinced that it would be too harsh a result in the circumstance. (52)

> If any prophylactic power remains in tort law, it would be strengthened by forcing entrepreneurs to pay for all the costs of their negligent activities, including some marginally foreseeable results, so that they will be stimulated to exercise greater care. In addition, perhaps an occasional award for a bizarre event will publicly dramatize the importance of safety measures. Lastly, general or market deterrence may be accomplished by transferring the entire cost of mishaps to the activity which produces them. (53)

These quotes probably push the envelope with regards to this concept, but they are cause for serious thought if you are a business owner!

Special Remoteness Problems for the Adventure Industry

There are a number of special remoteness problems that relate to the adventure industry — primarily those pertaining to the "thin-skull rule" and to the rescuer.

The thin-skull rule

The *thin-skull* rule refers to the legal principle that a defendant must take a plaintiff as he or she is found and that the defendant will be held liable for the entire extent of a plaintiff's injuries: "One who is guilty of negligence to another must put up with idiosyncrasies of his victim that increase the likelihood or extent of damage to him — it is no answer to a claim for a fractured skull that its owner had an unusually fragile one." (54)

The most common thin-skull problem is when a victim has a *pre-existing condition*: "If the injury proves more serious in … its consequences because of the injured man's condition, that does nothing but increase the damages the defendant must pay." (55) Thin-skull rulings are frequent, and the principle has been applied to pre-existing skeletal injuries, (56) heart conditions, (57) high blood pressure (58) and obesity, (59) among many others.

The thin-skull rule has implications for adventure businesses and the manner in which they use medical and disclosure forms. These forms are intended as screening tools to determine pre-existing conditions and should be applied as such. They serve little usefulness except in proving to a court that the business knew of the condition prior to a subsequent injury. "This would clearly work against a defense unless the business refuses participants based upon a pre-existing condition or the participant did not disclose the condition." (60)

The duty to rescuers

A negligent defendant may be held liable for injuries to a rescuer. For example, if a client is injured while under the care of a guide and a rescuer attempts a rescue and is injured during the attempt, the guide may be liable for injuries to the rescuer. (61)

> Danger invites rescue. The cry of distress is the summons to relief. The law does not ignore these reactions of the mind in tracing conduct to its consequences. It recognizes them as normal. It places their effects within the range of the natural and probable. The wrong that imperils life is a wrong to the imperiled victim; it is a wrong also to his rescuer.… The wrongdoer may not have foreseen the coming of a deliverer. He is accountable as if he had. (62)

Although no duty exists for an outside person to attempt a rescue, once a rescue has been initiated, the victim (and the guiding business) may be liable for injury to the rescuer.

In order for the defendant to be liable for a rescuer's injuries, the situation must have been created by the defendant's negligent actions. This does not mean, however, that the original victim who is the object of the rescue needs to be able to sue the defendant, since the defendant may have no duty to the victim (as in the case of trespass) (63) or the victim may be the cause of the accident (contributory negligence).

The rescue does not need to be successful: "in fact, it may have been futile from the outset. As long as the rescue attempt was not reckless and foolhardy … or [the rescuer] negligent in causing their own harm." (64)

In cases where the victim may be liable for a rescuer's injuries, there need not be actual danger to the victim but a reasonable belief that the person was in danger, (65) and the victim may already be dead. (66) The rescuer must not act in a "rash or reckless" (67) manner, and a rescuer's settlement may be reduced due to contributory negligence. (68)

> Even during an attempt to assist someone in an emergency, the law expects reasonable care to be exercised, even though the standard is relaxed to a certain extent. The court does not expect perfection, but rescuers must be sensible. They, like anyone else, must weigh the advantages and risks of their conduct. Their conduct too, however laudable, must measure up to the standard of the reasonable person in similar circumstances. (69)

Professional rescuers (and quite possibly volunteer rescuers acting as agents of an organized rescue party) may also sue a negligent party for personal injury (70) or property loss. (71) A possible condition here is that the injuries to a professional rescuer not arise from an exceptional risk; as long as the professional was carrying out his or her normal duties in a skillful manner, he or she will be treated like other rescuers. There may be public policy (municipal, provincial or federal) that discourages the professional rescuer from suing a victim, but there appears to be nothing in negligence law which prevents it. However, in order to receive workers' compensation after an injury, the professional rescuer may have to sign away his or her rights to further legal action against the victim or the employer. This is the case for volunteer search-and-rescue personnel acting on behalf of the Provincial Emergency Program in British Columbia.

Occupier Liability

Occupier liability is the branch of tort law which deals with the potential liability of those who control land towards those who enter the property. Historically, this branch of law categorized persons entering property as trespassers, licensees, invitees or contractual entrants — and applied different standards of care to each. Over time, the courts have merged these categories into persons who enter the premises on lawful grounds and persons who are trespassers. Guests of adventure operators enter lawfully, often under contract; as a contractual entrant, a guest has paid for the right to enter the premises.

Occupier-liability statutes determine the care required of an occupier towards the safety and property of persons entering the premises. An occupier of premises owes a duty to take reasonable care to ensure that a person and his or her property, while on the premises, will be reasonably safe in using those premises. This duty of care refers to the condition of the premises, any activities on the premises and the conduct of third parties on the premises. Occupier-liability statutes define an occupier as anyone who:

> [is] in physical possession of premises, or has responsibility for, and control over, the condition of premises, the activities conducted on those premises and the persons

allowed to enter those premises. There may be more than one occupier of the same premises. A premises includes lands and structures, excepting portable structures, ships and vessels, trailers and portable structures designed or used for a residence, business or shelter, and railway locomotives and cars, vehicles and aircraft while not in operation. (72)

This definition may vary between jurisdictions. Rivers, mountains and oceans are generally not considered premises.

An occupier normally will have no duty of care to a person who willingly accepts risks associated with entering the premises, who enters as a trespasser, who creates a danger with intent to do harm or to damage the property or who acts recklessly and disregards his or her own safety. An exception arises when a defendant creates what is considered an "attraction" (a good example of this is a swimming pool in a residential backyard), as it is foreseeable that people (even if they are trespassers) will be drawn to this attraction. Examples of attractions created by adventure businesses include climbing walls, high ropes courses, and bridges built for bungee jumping.

Many jurisdictions allow an occupier (this might include a permit holder) to restrict his or her liability through an express agreement with the person entering the premises. Release documents used by adventure operators may attempt to do this, and many include a specific statement that refers to an *Occupier Liability Act*. For example, many waivers in the snow-cat- and heli-ski industry say the following in their release language:

> To release the operator from any and all liability for any loss, damage, expense or injury including death that I may suffer or that my next of kin may suffer as a result of my participation in wilderness skiing, DUE TO ANY CAUSE WHATSOEVER, INCLUDING NEGLIGENCE, BREACH OF CONTRACT, OR BREACH OF ANY STATUTORY OR OTHER DUTY OF CARE, INCLUDING ANY DUTY OF CARE OWED UNDER THE OCCUPIER'S LIABILITY ACT, R.S.B.C. C. 1996, c. 337, ON THE PART OF THE OPERATOR. (73)

Notes to Chapter Two

1. Linden, *Canadian Tort Law*, 5th edition (1993), at 1, citing Fleming, *The Law of Torts*, 6th edition (1983), at 1.
2. Klar, *Tort Law* (1993), at 110, citing *Blyth v. Birmingham Waterworks Co.* (1869), L.R. 5 Exch.1.
3. Klar, *Tort Law* (1993), at 114, citing Lord Atkin in *Donahue v. Stevenson*, [1932] A.C. 562 (H.L.).
4. Keith Parkhari (Attorney at Law), editing comments, March 2000.
5. Madame Justice Wilson in *Crocker v. Sundance Northwest Resorts Ltd.* (1988), 44 C.C.L.T. 225, at 78.

6. Chief Justice Laskin in *Jordon House Ltd. v. Menow* (1973), 38 D.L.R. (3d) 105, at 111.

7. See *Lapensee v. Ottawa Day Nursery Inc.* (1986), 35 C.C.L.T. 129.

8. See: *McKay v. Bd. of Govan School Unit #29*, [1968] S.C.R. 589; *Dziwenka v. R.*, [1972] S.C.R. 419; *Thornton v. Prince George Board of School Trustees* (1978), 3 C.C.L.T 257; *Myers v. Peel County Board of Education* (1981), 17 C.C.L.T. 269; *Smith v. Horizon Aero Sports Ltd.* (1981), 19 C.C.L.T. 89; and others.

9. See *Poppe v. Tuttle* (1980), 14 C.C.L.T. 115.

10. See *Horsley v. Maclaren* (1969), 2 O.R. 137, reversed (1970), 2 O.R. 487, affirmed 22 D.L.R. (3d) 545.

11. See *Stermer v. Lawson* (1980), 11 C.C.L.T. 76.

12. See *Zelenko v. Gimbel Brothers* (1936), 287 N.Y.S.

13. Klar, *Tort Law*, at 142, citing *East Suffolk Rivers Catchment Bd. v. Kent*, [1940] 4 All E.R. 527 (H.L.).

14. See *Goldman v. Hargrave* (1967), 3 U.B.C.L. Rev 211.

15. *Buch v. Amory Mfg. Co.* (1898), 69 N.H. 257.

16. Chief Justice Jessup, Court of Appeal, in *Horsley v. MacLaren* (1970), 2 O.R. 487, at 499.

17. Ibid.

18. Klar, *Tort Law*, at 128.

19. Linden, *Canadian Tort Law*, at 266.

20. Willes, *Contemporary Canadian Business Law*, 4th edition (1994), at 86.

21. Baron Alderson in *Blyth v. Birmingham Water Works. Co.* (1856), 11 Ex. 781, at 784; 156 E.R. 1047.

22. See *Vaughan v. Menlove* (1837), 3 Bing, N.C. 468, at 475; 132 E.R. 490.

23. See *Mt. Isa Mines v. Pusey* (1971), 45 A.L.J.R. 88.

24. See *Armond v. Carr*, [1926] S.C.R. 575, at 581.

25. *Ouellet v. Cloutier*, [1947] S.C.R. 521, at 526.

26. Lord MacMillan in *Glasgow Corporation v. Muir*, [1943] A.C. 448, at 457.

27. See *Hedley Byrne & Co. v. Heller & Partners*, [1963] 2 All E.R. 575 (H.L.).

28. Don Blakely (Attorney at Law), communication, February 21, 2000.

29. Lord Edmund-Davies in *Whitehouse v. Jordan*, [1981] 1 W.L.R. 246 (C.A.).

30. Klar, *Tort Law*, at 235. See also *Maynard v. West Midlands Regional Health Authority*, [1984] 1 W.L.R. 634.

31. See *Quintal v. Datta*, [1988] 6 W.W.R. 481 (Sask. C.A.).

32. Don Blakely (Attorney at Law), communication, February 21, 2000.

33. Justice Callaghan in *Hahgato v. London Health Assn.* (1982), 36 O.R. (2d) 669, at 693 (H.C.).

34. Klar, *Tort Law*, at 210.

35. See: *Crits v. Sylvester*, 1 D.L.R. (2d) 502, affirmed [1956] S.C.R. 991; and *Wilson v. Swanson* (1956), 5 D.L.R. (2d) 113 (S.C.C.).

36. See *Central & Eastern Trust Co. v. Rafuse* (1986), 37 C.C.L.T. 117 (S.C.C.).

37. Justice Megarry in *Duchess of Argyll v. Beuselinck*, [1972] 2 Lloyd's Rep. 172, at 183.

38. Klar, *Tort Law*, at 239.

39. Klar, at 240.

40. See *Rayner v. Knickle* (1988), 47 C.C.L.T. 141 (P.E.I. S.C.).

41. See: *Reibl v. Hughes* (1980), 14 C.C.L.T. 1 (S.C.C.); and *Hopp v. Lepp* (1980), 13 C.C.L.T. 66 (S.C.C.).

42. Linden, *Canadian Tort Law*, at 153.

43. See *Haughian v. Paine* (1987), 40 C.C.L.T. 13 (Sask. C.A.).

44. See *Zambro v. Brisson* (1981), 16 C.C.L.T. 66 (Ont. C.A.).

45. See *Weiss v. Solomon* (1989), 48 C.C.L.T. 280 (Que. S.C.).

46. Linden, *Canadian Tort Law*, at 154.

47. See *Myers v. Peel County Board of Education* (1981), 123 D.L.R. (3d) 1 (S.C.C.).

48. See *Barker v. Permanent Seamless Floors Pty. Ltd.* (1983), 2 Qd. R. 561, among others.

49. Klar, *Tort Law*, at 269.

50. Linden, *Canadian Tort Law*, at 321.

51. Klar, *Tort Law*, at 279.

52. Linden, *Canadian Tort Law*, at 321.

53. Linden, at 323.

54. Lord Justice MacKinnon in *Owens v. Liverpool*, [1939] 1 K.B. 394, at 400.

55. Justice Dixon in *Watts v. Rake* (1960), 108 C.L.R. 158, at 160 (H.C. Aus.).

56. See *Peacock v. Mills and the City of Calgary* (1964), 50 W.W.R. 626 (Alta. C.A.).

57. See *Williams v. B.A.L.M. Ltd.* (1951), N.Z.L.R. 893.

58. See *Barnaby v. O'Leary* (1956), 5 D.L.R. (2d) 41.

59. See *Diederichs v. Metropolitan Stores Ltd.* (1956), 6 D.L.R. (2d) 751.

60. Keith Parkhari (Attorney at Law), editing comments, March 2000.

61. See, among others: *Horsley v. Maclaren*, [1972] S.C.R. 441; *Moddejonge v. Huron County Board of Education* (1972), 2 O.R. 437 (H.C.); and *Corothers v. Slobodian*, [1975] 2 S.C.R. 633.

62. Linden, *Canadian Tort Law*, at 335, quoting Justice Cardozo in *Wagner v. International Railroad Co.* (1921), 232 N.Y. Supp. 176, 133 N.E. 437.

63. See *Videan v. Br. Tpt. Comm.*, [1963] 2 Q.B. 650 (C.A.).

64. See *Cleary v. Hansen* (1981), 18 C.C.L.T. 147, at 155 (Ont. H.C.).

65. See *Ould v. Butler's Wharf*, [1953] 2 Lloyd's Rep. 44

66. See: *Haigh v. Grand Trunk Pacific Railway Company*, [1914] 7 W.W.R. (N.S.) 806 (Alta.); *Seymour v. Winnipeg Electric Railway Company*, [1910] 13 W.L.R. 566; *Woods v. Caledonian Railway* (1886), 23 S.L.R. 798; and *Moddejonge v. Huron County Board of Education* (1972), 2 O.R. 437, at 444.

67. See *Wagner v. International Railway* (1921), 232 N.Y. Supp. 176, 133 N.E. 437.

68. See: *Toy v. Argenti*, [1980] 3. W.W.R. 276, at 284; and *Horsley v. MacLaren* (1969), 2 O.R. 137, affirmed (1972), 22 D.L.R. (3d) 545; among others.

69. *Cleary v. Hansen* (1981), 18 C.C.L.T. 147, at 156.
70. See *Ogwo v. Taylor*, [1987] 3 E.R. 961 (H.L.).
71. See *Thorn v. James* (1903), 14 Man. R. 373.
72. *Occupier's Liability Act*, R.S.B.C. C. 1979, c. 303, Section 1.
73. The capital letters are as found in most releases.

Chapter Three

Defenses to Negligence

*A*lthough the plaintiff may have proved a required duty and standard of care and a subsequent breach of that duty, his or her claim may still be unsuccessful. It was stated in Chapter Two, in the discussion about the elements of a negligent action, that there should be no factors in the plaintiff's conduct which justify a reduction or an elimination of the damages awarded — such as voluntarily assuming the risk, signing an express agreement or being guilty of contributory negligence.

Contributory negligence and voluntary assumption of risk are both defenses that attempt to prove that the plaintiff's own conduct should reduce or eliminate liability on the part of the defending party. They are used extensively throughout the adventure industry, and their success often depends on a combination of educational, warning and contractual actions undertaken by the adventure business and its employees.

The legal rationale behind these defenses is that if a plaintiff's own actions limit the liability of the business, the plaintiff's right to recourse is limited by those actions. Apportionment laws typically reduce the amount of any settlement by the portion for which the plaintiff's actions are responsible — up to one hundred per cent of the claim. In the case of an express agreement such as a waiver, the plaintiff's actions may act as a complete defense.

In Canada, contributory negligence is used as a defense, whereas voluntary assumption of risk requires an explicit agreement, i.e. the inclusion of release language. In the United States, however, voluntary assumption of risk acts as a complete defense (*see Chapter Seven*).

Contributory Negligence

A plaintiff has the duty to take reasonable care to prevent injury to him or herself. Contributory negligence is conduct on the part of the plaintiff which is deemed by the courts to have been unreasonable and to have contributed to his or her own harm. The fact that plaintiffs have a duty to themselves to look after their own safety is entrenched in legislation adopted by every Canadian province and by many American states; although the wording may vary, the intent is the same.

If contributory negligence is proved, the plaintiff's compensation will be reduced. In theory at least, the standard of care required of a plaintiff for him or herself is the same as that to which the defendant will be held. This is frequently not the case, however, and plaintiffs are often treated more leniently than defendants. This may be especially the case in emergency situations or if the defendant is an expert or specialist: "A person placed in a perilous position cannot be required to exercise as much judgement and self-control in attempting to avoid danger as would reasonably be expected of him under ordinary circumstances." (1)

What is important is not whether the plaintiff's negligence contributed to the original accident but whether it contributed to the injuries, which can occur in one of three ways: "The plaintiff's negligence may: 1) contribute to the accident itself, 2) consist in the plaintiff's self-exposure to a risk of involvement in an accident, or 3) consist in the failure to take precautions to prevent or minimize possible injuries should an accident occur." (2)

There have been many cases where plaintiffs were held to contribute to their own injuries. For example: A heli-ski client who died in an avalanche was found contributorily negligent for disobeying a guide's instructions; (3) and boaters contributed to their own drowning, in one case by not wearing life jackets (4) and in another case by not keeping a boat in control and a proper lookout for a waterfall. (5) Contributory negligence was found against an individual for being drunk and participating in a tubing race, (6) against a snowmobile passenger for not warning the driver about not being seated safely (7) and against a golfer for standing where he was and not warning another golfer that he was there. (8)

One of the highest-profile contributory negligence cases in recent years was that of *Scurfield v. Cariboo Helicopter Skiing Ltd.* (9) Ralph Scurfield, a Calgary millionaire and part-owner of the Calgary Flames, died along with Mr. Randall Broyhill of Arlington, Virginia, in a 1985 avalanche while heli-skiing near Blue River, B.C. The B.C. Supreme Court ruled that Mr. Scurfield was 75-per-cent responsible for his death, and that Cariboo was 25-per-cent responsible for the accident because it took a party of skiers into a known avalanche area. The company was ordered to pay $1.1 million to Mr. Scurfield's widow.

The Scurfield family appealed, asking the Court to raise Cariboo's level of responsibility and to increase the damages. However, a trio of judges at the British Columbia Court of Appeal responded in January of 1993 by dismissing the appeal and ruling that Mr. Scurfield had taken several unnecessary risks and should be held entirely responsible for his own death. Cariboo was not required to pay anything to the Scurfield family.

In their decision, the appeal judges noted that Mr. Scurfield had disobeyed his guide's orders by entering the avalanche area before another skier had finished traversing it. It was ruled that "the cause of his death was his failure to follow the ski alert rule — to heed the danger of which he had been amply warned, which he could clearly see ahead and to which his attention was called." (10)

Voluntary Assumption of Risk

The defense of voluntary assumption of risk is possible when there is an agreement between two or more parties (business and client) that they will participate in an activity involving a degree of risk and that the client will give up his or her right to sue in the event that an injury results from that risk: "No act is actionable as a tort at the suit of any person who has expressly or impliedly assented to it." (11) This defense is otherwise known as *volenti non fit injuria*, or *volenti*. Voluntary assumption of risk must be pleaded and proved by the defendant. (12)

Theoretically, if successful, a defense of *volenti* in the United States may completely protect a defendant from liability. In Canada, however, such an argument has not been effective for many years — unless the agreement is expressly agreed to, which requires a written legal release. At this point, the defense is based on the release language in the document and not on the assumption-of-risk language.

In Canada, the assumption-of-risk language in a waiver still contains merit because of its educational and context-placing value. However, without release language in a waiver, a case would need to be defended on the basis of lack of negligence on the part of the operator rather than on the basis of assumption of risk on the part of the client.

The concept of voluntary assumption of risk stems from the court's views that "anyone should be able to work out one's destiny without interference from the law ... that people who consent to run the risk of injury do not deserve the protection of the law ... and that if someone willingly assumes the risk of an accident, a defendant should be shielded from responsibility." (13)

The agreement made between the parties may be made in writing, in words or in conduct, but it must be made prior to the activity:

> [In such an agreement,] the plaintiff, knowing of the virtually certain risk of harm, is in essence bargaining away his right to sue for injuries incurred as a result of any negligence on the defendant's part. The acceptance of the risk ... will arise only where there can truly be said to be an understanding on the part of both parties that the defendant assumed no responsibility to take due care for the safety of the plaintiff, and the plaintiff did not expect him to. (14)

In the adventure industry, the most common method of creating this type of defense is done proactively through the use of a legal-release form. This contractual agreement is a pre-emptive attempt by the defendant to relieve him or herself of an otherwise existing legal duty to take reasonable care for the plaintiff's protection. The rationale here is that a defendant cannot be held liable for acting in the manner that was foreseen and agreed to by the parties.

In such cases, the court will want to be absolutely clear that the plaintiff knew of the nature and risks of the activity and agreed to assume those risks. Thus, notwithstanding the use of tools such as a legal release, there is onus on the defendant to clearly be able to demonstrate success in educating the plaintiff with regard to the scope and scale of the potential risks and in providing a method for the plaintiff to voluntarily accept those risks. In addition, the plaintiff must be able to say no to the risks. This highlights the importance of the content and style of educational materials and safety talks provided by an adventure business to its guests. A defense of voluntary assumption of risk is unlikely to work if it is proved in court that a plaintiff was uncertain of the risks, was pressured into saying yes, did not understand the terms of the agreement or was not provided the opportunity to say no.

An agreement to accept the risks of an activity may be made *expressly* or *implicitly*. (15)

Express Agreements
An express agreement can be entered into as part of a contractual agreement. In the adventure industry, this happens most often when a legal release, or waiver, is signed by clients. The validity of these releases will be determined as a matter of contract law.

As part of an express agreement, the plaintiff typically agrees to "hold harmless" the defendant from all legal claims for damages stemming from participating in the activity. This may even go so far as to exclude negligence on the part of the defendant. "Express agreements must be clear, brought to the other [party's] attention, adequate for the purpose for which they are intended and agreed to by the parties." (16) *See Chapter Six for more on express agreements.*

Implied Agreements

In cases where there is no express agreement, the conduct of the two parties may imply an agreement. In such an event, it could be determined that the plaintiff had voluntarily assumed the risks associated with the activity.

It is difficult to predict with certainty in which cases a court will determine that an implied agreement deprives a victim of any compensation. However, it is clear that such a decision will be resisted by the courts and will be a bit of a stretch for most of them. The success of such a defense will depend on the courts deciding that one could "legitimately infer from the conduct of *both parties* that the plaintiff had impliedly agreed to waive the defendant's legal responsibility for injuries which might result from ... the activity." (17) Note the emphasis on the conduct of both parties. This is not something the defense can imply unilaterally; it will be determined by the behaviour of both parties in a bilateral manner: "Canadian law now requires proof that a bilateral bargain was actually made, expressly or by necessary implication from the facts, with the onus on the defendant to advance such proof, a burden especially difficult to discharge in ... gross negligence cases." (18)

It is clear from court rulings in implied-agreement cases that the defense is rarely successful. (19) This stems primarily, although not exclusively, from the distinction between the plaintiff's acceptance of the physical risks and his or her acceptance of the legal risks. Physical risk is defined as the risk of damage, whereas legal risk is the risk of damage for which there will be no legal redress. (20) For a defense of implied agreement to be successful, it must be proved that "the plaintiff voluntarily assumed the risk and ... accepted both the physical and legal risk." (21) Without a written, express agreement containing strong release language, this would be very hard for the defense to achieve.

Apportionment

Apportionment is the ability of a court to divide liability among those parties at fault — even when the plaintiff is found contributorily negligent. All Canadian provinces and many American states have adopted apportionment legislation through either a *Contributory Negligence Act* or a *Negligence Act*; although these acts may differ in their wording, their essence and intent remain the same: "When by fault of two or more persons damage or loss is caused to one of them, the liability to make good the damage or loss is in proportion to the degree in which each person was at fault...." (22)

For example: Assume a plaintiff is found to be 75 per cent at fault and the defendant 25 per cent at fault (as in the Scurfield case referred to above). The plaintiff (or his or her estate) is entitled to 25 per cent of the losses suffered. So, if the value of the loss were determined to be $4.4 million, the plaintiff would be found at fault for $3.3 million and the defendant would still need to pay the plaintiff $1.1 million for the defendant's share of the loss.

Although cases involving multiple parties are more complicated, a similar format is used for determining judgements. For example: Assume a plaintiff is found to be 25 per cent at fault, the defendant adventure-business operator is found to be 50 per cent at fault and the defendant government landowner who issued an operating permit to the business operator is found to be 25 per cent at fault. The same $4.4 million loss would find the plaintiff at fault for $1.1 million, the business operator at fault for $2.2 million and the government landowner at fault for $1.1 million. So, the plaintiff would receive $3.3 million in total, paid by the business owner and the government landowner. As is typical with most land-use permits, it is likely that the government would have required the business operator to name the government (the Crown) in its insurance policy in order to have the business pay for any losses for which the government may be found at fault.

In apportionment judgements, the parties may be found liable in any proportion. For example, plaintiffs and multiple defendants may be held equally at fault; (23) four different parties may be held equally to blame; (24) a plaintiff may be held 87.5 per cent to blame and the defendant 12.5 per cent; (25) judgements may apportion 10 per cent to the defendant, 15 per cent to the plaintiff and 75 per cent to no one; (26) and apportionment may be applied to other forms of tort (in this case, nuisance). (27)

Vicarious Liability

A party is vicariously liable when the liability is not based on wrongdoing by the party itself but on the conduct of someone else. The liability arises from the relationship between the party and the person who is involved in conduct that creates liability. The first party is held liable for the conduct of the second party's actions.

In the adventure industry, vicarious liability is primarily applied to employer/employee relationships where an employer is held responsible for the tortious actions of an employee. An employer may be vicariously liable for the actions of an employee during the course of his or her employment but may not be held liable for actions that were not sanctioned by the employer or that were beyond the scope of the employee's employment. This is based on the court's position that losses caused by an activity should be placed on the person who benefits from that activity the most and who has the ability to pay for the loss. Presumably, this is the employer. In some situations, however, it is still possible for an employee to be required to indemnify the employer for losses paid due to the employee's actions. (28)

One reason adventure-industry employers use a large number of contracted employees is that they are attempting to create an "arm's-length" relationship with the worker and to establish a "contract for service" relationship. Contractor hiring takes place for two main reasons: to simplify hiring and save costs; and, more relevant to this discussion, to try to transfer employer liability to the worker.

Contractor or Employee?

A worker may be hired on either a contract *of* service or a contract *for* service. A contract of service is where an employee is hired; a contract for service is where an independent contractor is hired. In order to determine whether or not to hold an employer vicariously liable, the court will depend extensively on establishing whether the worker was an employee or an independent contractor. To do this, a *control test* is applied. (29) *Control* refers to the degree of control over the worker and is defined as the employer telling the worker what to do and how to do it, whereas an independent contractor is hired to do a certain job without being told how to carry it out.

In addition to the control test, other questions deemed relevant by the courts are: "who owns the tools, stands the chance to profit or loss, whose business is it?" (30) As well: "[The] authority to fire, hire, suspend or reprimand, the manner of payment and the right of selection are also to be considered." (31) In other words, was the worker employed in relation to the employee's or the employer's business?

Although the above criteria appear straightforward, cases exist where an employer was held vicariously liable even when an employee disregarded express instructions, (32) when an employee carried out a deliberate wrong (33) and when an employee engaged in horseplay at work. (34)

The concept of vicarious liability for adventure operators takes an interesting twist when workers, including contractors, are involved in intrinsically dangerous activities: "It has been held in several judgements that where a person hires someone to engage in intrinsically dangerous work, the employer will be held liable if injury results from the negligent performance of that work." (35)

It is likely that the use of contracted workers is one of the most misunderstood aspects of the adventure industry. A large number of business owners "contract" their workers in order to save both money and administrative work, as well as in an attempt to transfer risk to the contractor. However, most "contractors" would not withstand the previously mentioned tests and the worker would be determined by the court to be an employee — regardless of the term used by the business or worker at the time.

Assessment of Damages

If the plaintiff is successful in proving his or her case, the court may rule not only that the defendant is liable for any injuries caused but that he or she must pay restitution to the plaintiff. The court determines the amount of damages, and money is awarded in an attempt to restore to the plaintiff what was lost as a result of the accident.

In order to assess the value of damages, the courts will consider the following types of categories:

- ❖ the injury itself and the pain and suffering associated with it up to the time of the judgement
- ❖ disability and loss of amenities before the judgement
- ❖ loss of earnings before the judgement
- ❖ expenses incurred before the judgement
- ❖ pain and suffering expected in the future
- ❖ loss of amenities after the judgement
- ❖ loss of earnings expected after the judgement
- ❖ the cost of future care and expenses
- ❖ the costs of defending the case

Notes to Chapter Three

1. Justice McKinnon in *Zervobeakos v. Zervobeakos* (1970), 8 D.L.R. (3d) 377, at 218 (N.S.C.A.).
2. Klar, *Tort Law* (1993), at 301, quoting Gravells, *Three Heads of Contributory Negligence* (1977), 93 L.Q.R. 581.
3. See *Scurfield v. Cariboo Heli-Skiing Ltd.* (1993), 74 B.C.L.R. (2d).
4. See *Chamberland v. Fleming* (1984), 29 C.C.L.T. 213 (Alta.).
5. See *Hendricks v. R.*, [1970] S.C.R. 237.
6. See *Crocker v. Sundance Northwest Resorts Ltd.*, [1988] 1 S.C.R. 1186.
7. See *Ainge v. Siemon* (1970), 3 O.R. 119.
8. See *Finnie v. Ropponen* (1987), 40 C.C.L.T. 155 (B.C.S.C.).
9. *Calgary Herald*, January 26, 1993.
10. *Scurfield v. Cariboo Heli-Skiing Ltd.* (1993), 74 B.C.L.R. (2d).
11. *Carnegie v. Trynchy*, [1966] 57 W.W.R. 305, at 308 (Alta.).
12. *McWilliam v. Thunder Bay Flying Club* (1950), O.W.N. 696, at p. 697.
13. Linden, *Canadian Tort Law*, 5th edition (1993), at 456.
14. Justice Estey in *Dube v. Labar* (1986), 36 C.C.L.T. 105, at 114 (S.C.C.).
15. Ibid.
16. Klar, *Tort Law*, at 321.
17. Klar, *Tort Law*, at 322.
18. Klar, *Tort Law*, at 324, quoting Chief Justice MacKeigan in *Crossan v. Gillis* (1979), 7 C.C.L.T. 269, reversed in 4 C.C.L.T. 184 (N.S.C.A.).
19. See: *Car & General Insurance Corp. v. Seymour & Maloney* (1956), 2 D.L.R. (2d) 369 (S.C.C.); and *Lehnert v. Stein* (1962), 36 D.L.R. (2d) 157 (S.C.C.).
20. Klar, *Tort Law*, at 323.
21. Justice Culliton in *Lackner v. Neath* (1966), 58 D.L.R. (2d) 662, 57 W.W.R. 496 (Sask. C.A.).

22. *Alberta Contributory Negligence Act*, s.1(1).

23. See *Menow v. Honsberger and Jordan House Ltd.* (1970), 1 O.R. 54, affirmed [1974] S.C.R. 239.

24. See *Teno v. Arnold* (1976), 11 O.R. (2d) 585 (C.A.).

25. See *Colonial Coach Lines v. Bennett and C.P.R.* (1968), 1 O.R. 333, 66 D.L.R. (2d) 396.

26. See *Houle v. B.C. Hydro and Power Authority* (1972), 29 D.L.R. (3d) 510.

27. See *Koch Industries Ltd. v. Vancouver*, [1982] 4 W.W.R. 92 (B.C.S.C.).

28. See, among others: *Lister v. Romford Ice and Cold Storage Ltd.*, [1957] A.C. 555; and *London Drugs Ltd. v. Kuehne & Nagel Int. Ltd.* (1990), 2 C.C.L.T. (2d) 161 (B.C.C.A.).

29. Klar, *Tort Law*, at 416.

30. See: *Montreal v. Montreal Locomotive Works Ltd.* [1946] 3 W.W.R. 748 (P.C.); and *McKee v. Dumas* (1976), 70 D.L.R. (3d) 70 (Ont.).

31. Klar, *Tort Law*, at 417.

32. See *Lockhart v. C.P.R.*, [1942] 3 W.W.R. 149 (P.C.).

33. See *Plains Engineering Ltd. v. Barnes Security Service Ltd.* (1987), 43 C.C.L.T. 129 (Alta. Q.B.).

34. See *Harrison v. Michelin Tyre Co.*, [1985] 1 All E.R. 918.

35. Klar, *Tort Law*, at 422, quoting, among others: *Bower v. Peate* (1876), 1 Q.B.D. 321; *Honeywell & Stein v. Larkin Brothers Ltd.*, [1934] 1 K.B. 191; and *Scarmar Construction Ltd. v. Geddes Contracting Ltd.* (1989), 61 D.L.R. (4th) 328 (B.C.C.A.).

Chapter
Four

Hospitality
Law

*I*n a text such as this, it is impossible to provide complete details regarding all aspects of relevant law. Many adventure operations service tourist clientele; when they do, several areas of hospitality law are applicable. This chapter is intended to provide an overview of law specific to tourism businesses and to create a general understanding of where to find additional hospitality-law information.

Legislation

Because tourism is a long-standing industry that includes such services as providing accommodation and serving food and liquor, many jurisdictions have extensive legislation that applies to businesses within this sector. It is necessary for operators to determine which parts of such legislation apply to them. Examples of appropriate legislation may include:

- ❖ *Hotel Keepers Act*
- ❖ *Hotel Guest Registration Act*
- ❖ *Hotel Tax Act*
- ❖ *Travel Regulation Act*
- ❖ *Tourism Act*
- ❖ *Travel Agents Act*
- ❖ *Consumer Protection Act*
- ❖ *Human Rights Act*
- ❖ *Employment Standards Act*

- ❖ *Workers' Compensation Act*
- ❖ *Company Act*
- ❖ *Health Act*
- ❖ *Labor Relations Code*
- ❖ *Liquor Control and Licensing Act*
- ❖ *Occupier's Liability Act*
- ❖ *Sale of Goods Act*
- ❖ *Social Services Tax Act*

Although it is difficult to generalize from one legal jurisdiction to another, common threads run through the legislation. Be sure to check your local statutes to compare with the following general observations.

Hotel and Innkeeper Legislation

Businesses that provide accommodation to guests may fall into the categories of hotel, innkeeper, bed and breakfast, resort, campground or recreational-vehicle park. Acts such as a *Hotel Keepers Act*, *Hotel Guest Registration Act* or *Hotel Tax Act* will apply to most accommodation providers. Campgrounds and recreational-vehicle parks do not normally fall under the category of hotels and are not included in many of the acts.

Such acts may include the following general themes:
- ❖ An operator must offer to accommodate guests provided that they are orderly and are willing to pay for the service. Accommodation facilities may refuse to accommodate a person who is unfit or disorderly or is unlikely to pay.
- ❖ An operator may place a lien on the property of a guest and sell the property for unpaid bills.
- ❖ There may be a limit on the operator's liability for a guest's property.

❖ An operator may evict a non-registered person who is considered undesirable.
❖ An operator must keep a guest register for all persons who are provided with accommodation.
❖ An operator may be required to collect "hotel tax" and submit it to the government.

The Yukon Wilderness Tourism Licensing Act

The *Yukon Wilderness Tourism Licensing Act* regulates the wilderness-tourism industry in the Yukon and is a unique piece of legislation in Canada. It came into effect on May 1, 1999. This act applies to anyone who takes clients into the Yukon wilderness when any kind of fee is involved.

The intent of the Act is "to sustain the wilderness quality of Yukon lands and waters, to require operators to obtain a license to conduct wilderness tourism activities, and by so doing, enhance the quality of the wilderness tourism sector".

In order to apply for the annual licence, the business must first have workers' compensation coverage for its employees and public-liability insurance for its clients, and the guides must have valid first-aid and CPR certificates. To renew the licence, the business must pay an annual fee, apply no-trace wilderness-travel techniques and submit trip and rental reports.

The Act defines no-trace travel techniques as those that:
❖ leave no more evidence of human activity than existed before the group arrived,
❖ use biodegradable soap products,
❖ pack out all unburned food,
❖ pack out all human solid waste or bury it at least 15 cm (6 in.) deep and 30 m (100 ft.) away from bodies of water, and
❖ pack out all used toilet paper or burn it completely in a campfire.

The Act requires that equipment rentals and day-trip and multi-day-trip group numbers be reported each year. Forms are provided for the requested information, which also includes trip type, secondary activities, trip location and duration, start and end dates, number of clients and their origin, and a report of any accidents.

Printed information accompanying the licence application clearly outlines immigration and work-permit laws for out-of-country businesses and provides information on trip sign-out for search-and-rescue purposes, as well as on First Nation land-claim negotiations.

Travel Agent, Wholesaler and Tour Operator Legislation

In some jurisdictions, tour operators are regulated under Travel Agent/Wholesaler/Tour Operator legislation. These laws vary from region to region and incorporate widely different approaches, but the development of legislation that applies to tour operators is definitely on the rise. In Canada, the provinces of British Columbia, Alberta, Ontario and Quebec all have similar legislation, while the *Wilderness Tourism Operators Act* in the Yukon is the only legislation specifically designed for adventure-tourism operations. In the United States, there are many variations on the same theme.

An example of such legislation is the *Travel Agents Act*, with its accompanying *Travel Agent Act Regulations*, found in the province of British Columbia. This act applies to businesses wishing to register as a travel agent, a travel wholesaler or a tour operator within British Columbia. Many tour operators do not realize that this legislation applies to them. Those who have gone through the entire process have been less than enthusiastic about it; many don't bother. Highlights of this act and the accompanying regulations are as follows:

✣ An "inbound" tour operator doing business in British Columbia is required to be registered under the *Travel Agents Act* and is subject to the Assurance Fund Levy, even when all of the travellers are resident in some other jurisdiction.

✣ The applicant must have a positive net-worth position and a positive working-capital position, supported by financial statements and an opening balance sheet.

✣ A corporation must have a minimum net-worth position of at least $15,000. Corporate net worth is determined as share capital plus retained earnings minus intangible assets/goodwill. Shareholder loans are a liability and are subtracted from net worth.

✣ All businesses and trade/business names must be registered with the British Columbia Registrar of Companies.

✣ Travel Agent registrations are non-transferable and expire on a change of ownership of the business.

✣ The retail applicant must provide and maintain an irrevocable letter of credit, naming the Registrar of Travel Services as the beneficiary, for a minimum of $15,000 plus $5,000 for each branch location. Tour operators and wholesalers should contact the Registrar for letter-of-credit requirements, as these are individually determined.

✣ An applicant must have two years' travel-industry experience gained in the previous five years.

✣ A registrant must operate from commercial premises and may not operate from a residence.

✣ The applicant must open, operate and maintain a consumer trust account at his or her financial institution.

✣ There is an application fee and an annual licence fee.

✣ A registrant must file a copy of his or her annual financial statement within 90 days of the business' fiscal year-end.

Adventure-program Legislation in Great Britain
An Example of Reactionary Legislative Development

*I*n Great Britain, what has become known as "the Lyme Bay incident" resulted in the passing of the *Activity Centres (Young Persons' Safety) Act* 1995. This act legislates a licensing authority to oversee the accreditation and licensing of providers of facilities for adventure activities.

In March of 1993, four teenagers died on an ocean canoe trip organized by an outdoor-education centre in Lyme Bay operated by OLL Ltd. (also known as St. Albans Centre). The staff did not check the weather forecast, the students had been given only one hour of canoe instruction before the trip, no distress flares were carried, whistles were the only safety equipment on hand, and the instructors were inexperienced. Prior to the disaster, two instructors had left the company over safety concerns, and one of the instructors had made these concerns known to the company manager in a letter.

Criminal prosecution for manslaughter on the basis of unlawful killing was brought against the director of OLL Ltd., the manager of the adventure centre where the accident occurred, and OLL Ltd. itself.(1) The company became the first in English legal history to be convicted of the common-law crime of manslaughter (death resulting from gross negligence), and it was fined £60,000. The director became the first director of a company to be given an immediate jail sentence for manslaughter conviction. He was found guilty of manslaughter by gross negligence on the basis of failing to establish proper safety procedures and was sentenced to two years' imprisonment. The jail sentence was passed despite the acceptance of the court that the director was unaware that school children were undertaking trips of the kind that resulted in the accident — in other words, he had no criminal intent.

Following the Lyme Bay incident, legislation was passed in June 1995 as the *Activity Centres (Young Persons' Safety) Act* 1995. The Act does not provide a definition of "facilities for adventure activities", but it expressly excludes facilities provided exclusively for people over the age of 18. The Act allows regulations to be made concerning who needs to obtain a licence and concerning safety requirements, the investigation of complaints and the bringing of appeals. The Act applies to anyone who provides adventure activities, for payment, to people under the age of 18. This includes individuals, municipalities, trusts and limited companies. The Act does not apply to volunteer groups. A private company was chosen as the licensing authority that implements the regulations.

A significant effect of the Act is to shift liability from directors, teachers and administrators to the provider of the adventure activity (guide and supervisor). The Act imposes criminal liability on providers of an adventure activity who fail to act in accordance with a licence or who knowingly make a false statement to the licensing authority. The punishment for an offence is a fine for a summary conviction, or a fine and/or up to two years' imprisonment for a conviction. (2)

The New Zealand No-fault Accident Insurance and Compensation System

An Example of Proactive Legislative Development

*T*he New Zealand government operates a 24-hour-a-day, no-fault accident insurance and compensation system for tourism operators. There is no right to sue for damages and no business liability for accidents. Under the *Accident Compensation Rehabilitation and Insurance (ARCI) Act* 1992, operators cannot be sued by their customers for compensatory damages arising directly or indirectly out of personal injury in cases where provision for that injury is provided under the *ARCI Act*.

Recent changes in the accident-compensation regime have seen a reduction in compensation levels and in some cases (such as lump-sum payments) a removal of previously available classes of compensation. As a result of these changes, the Australian Plaintiff Lawyers Association has called on Australian travellers to take out additional comprehensive medical insurance if they intend to take part in "high-risk" adventure activities while in New Zealand.

Under the *Consumer Guarantees Act* 1993, certain conditions are stipulated in the contract between the consumer and the activity provider, including a guarantee that the activity will be carried out with reasonable care and skill. A consumer could be granted damages if he or she suffered loss as a result of not receiving an appropriate level of care. However, such damages cannot be claimed for personal injury covered by the *ARCI Act*.

The prosecution of operators and organizations who are found negligent in protecting the safety of customers in their care is carried out under the *Crimes Act* 1961. (3)

❖ Registrants must implement trust-accounting techniques — where the money received from a traveller is held in a trust account until such time as the trip is operated, and the money held continues to be the beneficial property of the person who paid it (see your accountant about this one!).

Liquor Sales Legislation

In many jurisdictions, a number of statutes apply to businesses that sell liquor. Such legislation may state that licensees:

❖ must complete a prescribed training program before serving liquor.
❖ must not sell, give or supply liquor to a minor or permit a minor to consume liquor in their establishments.
❖ must not store, sell, or give liquor except in accordance with the applicable act.

✤ must not permit gambling, drunkenness or violence in a licensed location.

✤ must not sell or give liquor to an intoxicated person.

✤ must not permit a person to become intoxicated, nor permit an intoxicated person to remain where liquor is stored, sold, served or supplied.

✤ must not discriminate in liquor sales contrary to human-rights legislation.

✤ must accept that there is a duty of care required of a business that stores, sells or serves liquor in order to protect patrons and others from harm that may result from drinking.

Notes to Chapter Four

1. The manager of the adventure centre was acquitted on the direction of the judge when the jury failed to reach a verdict.
2. The above is taken from "Safety at Adventure Activities Centers Following the Lyme Bay Tragedy: What Are the Legal Consequences", by Yvonne Jacobs in *Education and the Law*, 8, 4 (December 1996). See also: the *Activity Centres (Young Person's Safety) Act* 1995 for the complete legislation; as well as "Guidance to the Licensing Authority on the Adventure Activities Licensing Regulations 1996" (U.K. Health and Safety Commission); and *A Report into Safety at Outdoor Activity Centres* (Sudbury, U.K., HSE Books, 1996).
3. Taken from "Safety Management in the Adventure Tourism Industry: Voluntary and Regulatory Approaches", the New Zealand Ministry of Commerce Web site, May 1996.

Chapter
Five

Contract
Law

Adventure-tourism businesses enter into a variety of contracts with other parties. These may include service agreements and legal releases with guests; agreements with accommodation and travel providers; insurance policies; employment contracts with contract workers; and agreements with travel agents and wholesalers.

A contract is a promise between two parties — the party promising (promisor) and the party to whom the promise is given (promisee) — to voluntarily undertake something. The promisor agrees to act (or not to act) in a certain way for the benefit of the promisee. The degree to which one party's promise is fulfilled or remains to be completed is the extent to which that party's side of the contract is completed. "A contract is a legally recognized agreement between two or more persons, giving rise to obligations to each other that may be enforced in the courts." (1) The court's role is to ensure that such an agreement is kept "in accordance to its letter and its spirit":

> By such an agreement the parties not only restrict their present or future freedom to act, by the limitations imposed upon themselves by the agreement, they are creating a legal rule, or set of legal rules, a legal regimen, binding as regards themselves and only themselves. It might be suggested that, through the device of contract, parties legislate for themselves, that is to say they create a miniature legal system by and under which they are governed. (2)

Agreement

For a contract to be valid, the parties need to be able to demonstrate that the agreement is intended to be taken seriously and not casually. In a business transaction, this is usually done through some form of "consideration" on the part of the promisee which demonstrates the agreement's serious nature. In adventure businesses, this is usually achieved by the exchange of money — for example, with a deposit. This could be from the client to the business or from a travel agent to a business, etc. "[F]or an agreement to be a contract, the promise must somehow have been 'bought' by the promisee." (3) Total payment is not necessary, and a deposit is sufficient consideration.

> Constantly reiterated in the judgements is the idea that the test of agreement for legal purposes is whether parties have indicated to the outside world, in the form of the objective reasonable bystander, their intention to contract and the terms of such a contract. It is not what an individual party believed or understood was the meaning of what the other party said or did that is the criterion of such an agreement; it is whether a reasonable man in the situation of that party would have believed and understood that the other party was consenting to the identical terms. (4)

Where there is a plainly worded document that has been signed by both parties, consensual agreement is relatively straightforward to determine. However:

> [I]f there is no single document to which reference can be made in order to decide if a contract exists between the parties, but a series of negotiations, then everything that occurs between the parties relevant to the alleged contract must be considered by the court which is faced with the problem of deciding the issue. (5)

and:

> Without an offer and its acceptance, there is no contract. If either or both is missing, there is no proof that the parties … had reached a stage in their negotiations in respect of which it could be said that they had shown not only an intent to be bound together, but the nature, extent, and manner of their being bound so as to give rise to a legally recognizable and enforceable contract. (6)

Capacity to Enter a Contract

In order to enter into a contract, the parties must be capable. This means that minors and those who are mentally incapable may not enter into contracts. It also means that capable persons as well as "artificial persons" such as corporations and societies may enter into contracts.

Minors

Although the age of majority varies from jurisdiction to jurisdiction, minors have limited capacity to enter into contracts. Stated in very simple terms, in most of Canada there are two categories of minor's contracts: those that are not valid and those where the law provides the minor the opportunity to opt out, if he or she chooses. In a contract with a minor, it is the minor's choice whether to enforce the contract (7) and: "As a general rule, minors' contracts should not be enforceable against them, but should be enforceable by them …." (8) However, even though the minor may choose to enforce a contract, "In many jurisdictions minors do not have standing in court and if they want to sue it must be done through a guardian or adult friend." (9)

Nonetheless, there may be exceptions to this: "[A minor] may bind himself to pay for his necessary meat, drink, clothing, medicines and likewise for his teaching and instruction." (10) This is intended to refer to items defined as "necessary goods", but how this is defined is unknown. In addition, a minor may bind him- or herself in an employment contract if it is for the minor's benefit and does not take advantage of the minor.

British Columbia, however, treats contracts with minors differently and regulates the capacity of minors to enter into contracts through a 1985 amendment to the *Infants Act*. In that province, a contract with a minor cannot be enforced against him unless:

a) the contract is enforceable against him by some statute, b) the minor affirms the contract on attaining majority, c) it is wholly or partially performed by the minor after majority, or d) it is not repudiated by the minor within a year after majority. However, the minor can enforce the contract against the adult party as if the minor had been an adult at the time of contracting. (11)

Business Corporations

Incorporated companies have the ability to enter into a contract in the same way as do individuals. They can also sue and be sued for terms having to do with the contract. If operating in a second province, a business will have to register in that province before appearing in court.

Unincorporated Associations

An unincorporated association has no separate corporate status, is not recognized by law and cannot contract. If the officers of an unincorporated association sign a contract on the association's behalf, they are personally liable. All the members of the association may be held "jointly and severally" liable for any liability the contract may bring the association.

Partnerships and Proprietorships

The principals in a partnership or proprietorship may contract, although they are not protected by any limited liability. The exception to this is the limited partner in a limited partnership, whose liability would normally be restricted to the amount of the original investment.

Contract Terms

Individuals entering into a contract will normally agree on the terms of the contract. A *term* is a statement in the contract that makes clear an obligation or set of obligations imposed on one or more of the parties to the contract. An *express term* is one that has been specifically mentioned, and agreed upon, by the parties. Such terms form the core of the contract and its intent. (12)

Contract terms do not need to be in writing. Written contracts are better than oral contracts, as written contracts make it easier for both the parties and the courts to prove what has been agreed to. However, once the courts determine what was said in an oral contract, this is what they will enforce. (13)

Where the language of the contract is clear, additional evidence will not be allowed to alter, vary or contradict the meaning of the contract, which will be given its literal meaning. (14) This is why the wording in release documents such as waivers, which the courts consider onerous, must be totally unambiguous. If the contract is not clear, additional evidence will be used to clarify its meaning.

"In cases of doubt, as a last resort, language should always be construed against the grantor or promisor under the contract." (15) This is known as the *contra proferentum* rule, which ensures that the meaning least favourable to the author of the document will prevail. (16) The *contra proferentum* rule "is also of great relevance where the contract being construed is a *contrat d'adhésion*, that is, where the signatory does not really have the opportunity to negotiate its terms but is obliged either to agree, and sign, or forgo whatever advantages such a contract might bring him." (17) This is describing a legal release exactly as it is used by the entire adventure-tourism industry in North America!

It is not always possible to restrict the terms of a contract to those expressly written in the document. Additional terms may be implied. Generally, however, the courts will be reluctant to go beyond the "letter" of the written contract unless there are strong reasons to do so.

Performance and Breach

There is a duty to complete a contract and to perform to its terms. Anything less than complete performance is a breach of the contract. The contract itself may contain language that clarifies the degree of strictness or flexibility allowed in the performance; for instance, the contract may dictate the time allowed for the performance to be completed or it may refer to how payment is to be made.

Technically, non-completion of a contract in any way is a breach of the terms of the contract; however, breach of any one condition in the contract does not completely nullify the remainder of the contract. Where it becomes impossible for one party to complete the contract, "the innocent party has the option to put an end to his obligations under the contract, holding himself no longer bound to perform the duties it places on him, or to maintain the binding quality of the contract as far as himself and the contract-breaker are concerned." (18) The innocent party is entitled to sue for damages related to his or her loss; or this party may choose to waive the breach, and the remainder of the terms of the contract may be completed by the contract breaker.

Exclusion Clauses

"Sometimes clauses are included in a contract for the purpose of protecting one party from total or partial liability to the other. A clause of this kind may exempt a party from all, or many forms of liability, for example negligence...." (19) These clauses are known as *exclusion clauses* and are intended to modify obligations within a contract and to exclude or limit one party's liability. (20) They are widely used within the adventure industry in legal releases.

Due to the onerous nature of such terms, "courts have adopted a stricter attitude towards such clauses...." (21) In addition, statutes have been passed in certain jurisdictions to limit exclusionary clauses in some contracts.

The courts are reluctant to allow a party to contract out of its own negligence:

[S]ince they have the effect of providing an advantage to one party as against the other, and because they are frequently inserted in contracts where one party has little opportunity to bargain with the party for whose benefit the clause is included ... the courts look very carefully at the validity, meaning and application of such clauses. (22)

For more detail regarding court judgements around exclusionary clauses, see Chapter Six.

The Right to Sue for Breach of Contract

When a contract has been broken, the innocent party is entitled to sue for damages related to his or her loss. The right to sue for breach of contract does not come from the contract itself but is a right given by law. The plaintiff does not have to prove that the breach was committed deliberately or negligently. If negligence was involved, there is the possibility that the plaintiff may undertake a tort action instead of an action for a breach of contract.

The right to sue for breach of contract may be waived by an exemption clause. In the adventure industry, this is often carried out by including such a clause in the legal release that is signed by clients.

There is a limit to the amount of time that may elapse while a party still has the right to sue. This limit is set by statute and, in Canada, is usually six years, although there are provisions that could lengthen this period. The limitation period starts at the time of the breach. (23)

Damages

"Where a party sustains a loss by reason of a breach of contract, he is, so far as money can do it, to be placed in the same situation, with respect to damages, as if the contract had been performed." (24) This may include the objective tests of expenses, loss of profits, loss of business, loss of earnings, loss of financial advantage, decrease in the value of goods or property, and physical injury to the person or to property. (25) In addition, compensation may be included for more intangible losses such as "loss of reputation, insult, annoyance, aggravation, nervous shock, inconvenience, mental distress or other emotional or sentimental suffering". (26)

Related to tourism: "[There have been claims] against travel agents who had broken contracts with their clients by sending them on holidays that turned out to be different from the promises made at the time the client bought the 'package.' As a consequence of this difference the client suffered inconvenience, distress, disappointment, aggravation, and the loss of the benefits that would have been expected from a successful holiday," (27) and: "Since those first instances of liability for such consequences, the courts have gradually extended the scope of such claims." (28)

Notes to Chapter Five

1. *Interprov. Concrete Ltd. v. Great West Const. Ltd.* (1987), 23 C.L.R. 123, at 130 (Sask. Q.B.).

2. Fridman, *The Law of Contract*, 3rd edition, at 5.

3. Justice McLellan in *Case's Insulation and Siding Ltd. v. Gordon* (1991), 45 C.L.R. 252, at 255 (N.B.Q.B.).

4. *I.T.T. Industries of Canada Ltd. v. Toronto Dominion Bank* (1988), 63 Alta. L.R. (2d) 87, at 307 (Alta. Q.B.).

5. *Baynes v. Vancouver Bd. of School Trustees* (1927), 2 D.L.R. 698, at 700 (B.C.S.C.).

6. Justice Hutchinson in *Bate Industrial Services Ltd. v. Enerflex Systems Ltd.* (1992), 132 A.R. 253, at 259 (Alta. Q.B.).

7. Fridman, *The Law of Contract*, at 142.

8. Ontario Law Reform Commission, *Report on Amendment of the Law of Contract*, 1987.

9. Keith Parkhari (Attorney at Law), editing comments, March 2000.

10. *Miller v. Smith & Co.*, [1925] 2 W.W.R. 360, at 377 (Sask. C.A.).

11. Fridman, *The Law of Contract*, at 157.

12. This paragraph is based on: Fridman, *The Law of Contract*, at 449.

13. Fridman, *The Law of Contract*, at 453.

14. *North Eastern Railway Co. v. Hastings*, [1900] A.C. 260 at 263 (H.L.).

15. Fridman, *The Law of Contract*, at 470, quoting *Milliken v. Young*, [1929] W.W.R. 213 (Sask. C.A.).

16. See *Huber v. Conquest Tours Ltd.* (1990), 74 O.R. 324 (Ont. H.C.), among others.

17. Fridman, *The Law of Contract*, at 471.

18. *Photo Production Ltd. v. Securicor Tpt. Ltd.*, [1980] 1 All E.R., at 556 (H.L.).

19. Fridman, *The Law of Contract*, at 571.

20. Ibid., quoting Justice Barry in *Howell v. Newfoundland* (A.G.) (1987), 65 Nfld. & P.E.I.R. 139, at 151 (Nfld. T.D.).

21. *Photo Production Ltd. v. Securicor Tpt. Ltd.*, [1980] 1 All E.R., at 567 (H.L.).

22. Fridman, *The Law of Contract*, at 572.

23. *Schwebel v. Telekes* (1967), 61 D.L.R. (2d) 470, at 474 (Ont. C.A.).

24. *Robinson v. Harman* (1848), 1 Ex. 850, at 855.

25. Fridman, *The Law of Contract*, at 721.

26. Fridman, *The Law of Contract*, at 736.

27. See: *Jarvis v. Sans Tours Ltd.*, [1973] 1 Q.B. 233 (C.A.); *Jackson v. Horizon Holidays Ltd.*, [1975] 3 All E.R. 92 (C.A.); *Keks v. Esquire Pleasure Tours Ltd.*, [1974] 3 W.W.R. 406 (Man. Co. Ct.); *Fuller v. Healey Tpt. Ltd.* (1978), 92 D.L.R. (3d) 277 (Ont Co. Ct.); *Pitzel v. Sask. Motor Club Travel Agency Ltd.* (1983), 149 D.L.R. (3d) 122 (Sask. Q.B.); and *Camerson v. Maritime Travel (Halifax) Ltd.* (1983), 58 N.S.R. (2d) 379 (N.S.T.D.).

28. Fridman, *The Law of Contract*, at 739.

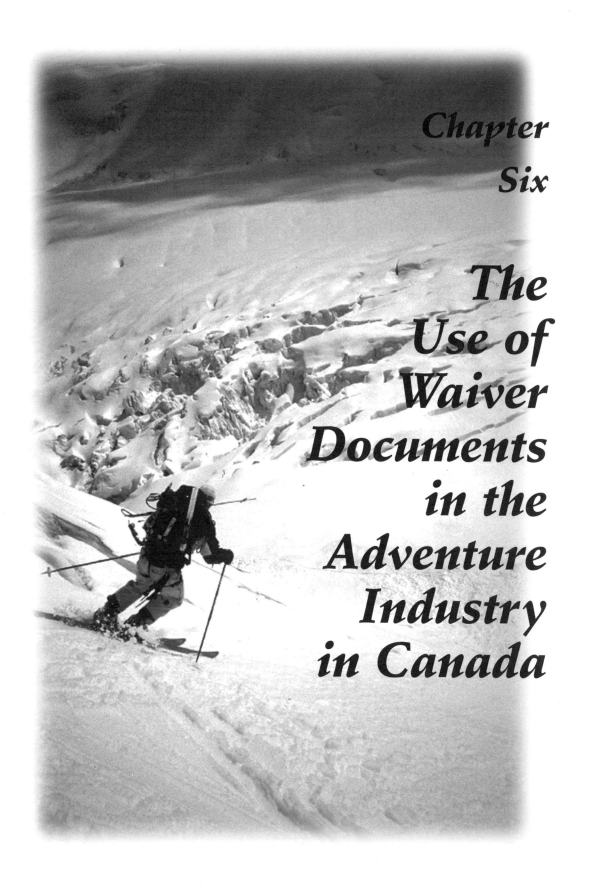

Chapter
Six

The Use of Waiver Documents in the Adventure Industry in Canada

*A*greements allocating legal risk to the user, commonly called *releases* or *waivers*, are often used as a form of express agreement in the adventure industry. Exclusionary terms printed on admission tickets, such as those sold at ski hills, are intended as the same. Risk management in adventure sports is more difficult than in some other fields because the risk of injury is dependent on individual behaviour in an unpredictable environment. These agreements are therefore used as a form of proactive risk management.

> The advantage a waiver holds for recreational operators is that it provides a contractual defense that is much more reliable than the fact-dependent tort defenses: exercise of reasonable care, contributory negligence, and assumption of risk (*volenti*). Where there is an enforceable contract excluding or limiting the operator's liability, it is decisive insofar as its terms extend. If the terms cover the accident in question and there is nothing in law to detract from their enforceability, a court will not look into the facts behind it to determine if liability should be imposed. (1)

Recent court judgements have consistently upheld the use of waivers by adventure operators, as well as supported their wide-ranging exclusionary terms. In spite of this reality, there is still significant confusion and misunderstanding on the part of many guides and operators as to the court's rationale and judgement regarding waivers. This chapter is intended to present a factual account of the evolution of waiver use as well as to provide the perspective of some recent court rulings.

Does the Release Bind the Plaintiff?

It is well known that an adventure operator's duty of care to a plaintiff is regulated by an *Occupier's Liability Act*. Such acts have a section that deals with the operator's ability to contract out of the duty that would generally be owed by the occupier. In British Columbia, Section 4 of the *Occupier's Liability Act*, R.S.B.C. C. 1996, c. 337, states: "Where an occupier is permitted by law to extend, restrict, modify or exclude his duty of care to any person by express agreement, or by express stipulation or notice, the occupier shall take reasonable steps to bring that extension, restriction, modification or exclusion to the attention of that person."

Provided that an adventure operator takes reasonable steps to bring a waiver to the attention of the plaintiff and that the document makes its identity clear and is presented and administrated adequately, the courts in Canada have a history of upholding waiver contracts. This applies to releases contained in the wording on ski-lift tickets as well as in more sophisticated signed contract documents used as waivers by operators. (2) The exceptions to this rule are when any of the following conditions apply:

❖ The document is signed by the plaintiff "in circumstances which make it not
   her act" (*non est factum*).
❖ The agreement has been induced by fraud or misrepresentation.

❖ The party seeking to enforce the document knew or had reason to know of the other's mistake as to its terms. (3)

Waiver Content

Most waivers are really a number of legal forms wrapped into one document. They often include content covering assumption of risk, waiver of claims, release of liability, and indemnification. The following components (and sometimes additional ones) might be part of a well-constructed waiver document:

❖ title (identity of the document)
❖ names of the two parties (*business and client*)
❖ definitions
❖ description of the activities included
❖ warning of risks
❖ acknowledgment and assumption of risks
❖ release of liability (waiver of claims)
❖ indemnity agreement
❖ binding on heirs and estate
❖ jurisdiction agreement
❖ reliance agreement
❖ legal-age statement
❖ agreement to waive right to sue
❖ signature
❖ witness

Delivering a Waiver

There are a number of principles that should be followed when delivering a release to a guest, including the following: (4)

❖ Provide advance notice that the guest will be required to sign a release. This notice should be included in the marketing and information packages received by the guest.
❖ Whenever possible, send the form in advance.
❖ Educate the guest regarding the contents of the release.
❖ The release should be written in clear, easy-to-understand terms.
❖ Provide time for the guest to read the release.
❖ Explain the terms in the release clearly.
❖ Provide an atmosphere that is conducive for the guest to read, understand and execute the release.
❖ Do not confuse the signing of the release with other signings that may be required.

✦ Make sure that the guest's signature is correct.

✦ Do not allow the guest to cross out or delete sections of the release.

✦ Have a witness sign the release, and collect his or her name and address. As the witness may have to provide evidence in court, he or she should be mature and responsible. The witness can be someone from the business.

✦ The release should be signed in front of the witness. The witness should ensure, by asking, that the guest understands the contents of the release.

✦ If the witness suspects that the guest is intoxicated, the witness should refuse to accept or witness the release.

✦ The guest should be provided with an opportunity to receive a copy of the release.

✦ Keep signed copies of the release and file them for not less than seven years from the end of the activity. The longer the period the better; in the case of a lawsuit, any releases signed by the guest for previous trips will be of value in establishing his or her knowledge levels and will help to prove an understanding of the document.

✦ Ensure that a control mechanism is in place to guarantee that no guest participates without signing the release.

✦ Do not attempt to interpret the waiver for the guest. If the guest requests an explanation of the meaning of the release, something along the following lines should be stated by the witness: "The document you are asked to sign is a release of liability. It is a legal document, and by signing the release you are giving up certain legal rights, including the right to sue should you be injured [or killed] during the event."

Specific and Comprehensive Waivers

Waivers may be designed to apply only to specific risks and sources of liability or to a broader and more comprehensive list of risks. A comprehensive waiver is designed so that an operator has no duty of care to clients and no obligation to compensate them for damages:

A comprehensive waiver used in the recreational sector typically contains a recitation that the participant recognizes the existence of inherent risks and dangers in the sport in question. It also states the user assumes all risks arising from participation in the sport and waives the operator from all claims of every kind, including those based on the operator's own negligence, breach of contract, and sometimes breach of statutory duty. Wording like this, drawn from an actual example, may be used:

I, for myself, my heirs, executors, administrators, or anyone else who may claim on my behalf, covenant not to sue, and waive, release, and discharge [operator, its employees, etc.] or anyone acting for or on their behalf, for any and all claims or liability for personal injury, death, damage to property or loss of whatsoever nature or kind and howsoever caused, whether arising by reason of the negligence of [operator, its employees, etc.] or otherwise. (5)

Indemnity clauses are also common in agreements. Under these, the user agrees to reimburse the operator for any damages the operator might become liable to pay to a third party as a result of the user's conduct.

Waivers by and on Behalf of Minors

A waiver is a legal contract, and "contracts made by minors are unenforceable."(6) It is common practice, however, to have minors sign a waiver before they are allowed to participate in certain athletic activities. The waiver form invariably contains a space for an additional signature by a parent. Sometimes the document takes the form of a waiver by the parent on behalf of the minor. This does not make it enforceable. (7) Parents cannot sign away the legal rights of their child.

Commercial recreational operators and amateur-sports associations obtain waivers from minors and their parents despite the fact they are unenforceable, because these waivers serve to draw both the minor's and the parent's attention to the possibility of injury, and afford some evidence that both are aware of and assume inherent risk.

In addition, despite the fact that a large portion of the general public seems to be aware that minors cannot make binding contracts, it is still possible that a parent may be deceived into thinking that a valid claim of a seriously injured minor cannot be pursued because of a waiver signed in connection with the minor's participation in some activity. (8)

This type of "bluffing" is neither ethical nor particularly legal and should be avoided by businesses.

Because voluntary assumption of risk is no longer a valid legal defense in Canada — for either minors or adults — cases involving minors must be defended based on the business not being negligent.

The Evolution of Waiver Documents

In England in the early 19th century, when the activity of the transportation industry increased dramatically, cargo and passenger carriers began, with the assistance of their lawyers, to look for methods of modifying the general law applicable to their carrying of goods and passengers. Companies sought to have customers enter into what were often called "special contracts" that could modify the common law or the decrees of statutes.

Due to the advent of the railway, cases involving waivers after the middle of the 19th century began to deal typically with railroad passengers. An example is *Van Toll v. Southeastern Railway Company*, (9) where in 1862 the railway was successful in upholding a waiver clause. In that case, the plaintiff, Van Toll, had deposited a bag containing clothing and jewelry in a storeroom at the railroad office and had received a ticket. In addition to the writing on the ticket, there was a prominent sign situated in the room where she had checked the items which stated that goods could be left but that the railway took no responsibility for them. Because it was ruled that the plaintiff had been given adequate notice, she was bound by the waiver. In 1876 came the case of *Harris v. Southeastern Railway Company*. (10) There, the railway passenger, who had deposited luggage with a clerk at the railway's storeroom and had received a ticket with limiting conditions, was also held to be bound by the notice limiting liability.

In the following year, the case of *Parker v. Southeastern Railway Company* (11) was decided; often quoted, it is usually considered to be a leading case in this area. Again, this case resulted from the deposit of goods in a storeroom at a railway station. The court ruled that, in order to successfully rely on a waiver or exemption clause as a defense, the defendant was obliged to have done what was reasonably necessary to give the customer adequate notice of conditions limiting liability.

In the case of *Hood v. Anchor Line* in 1918, (12) similar issues were faced in the context of steamship travel. There, a passenger bound for the United States from the United Kingdom sued for injuries he had suffered due to the negligence of the steamship company, which caused him harm when he was being transferred from a grounded ship to another ship off the Irish coast. The House of Lords upheld the earlier decision of the Scottish Court in favour of Union Steamships Ltd., on the basis that the passenger was bound by the limitations of liability written on the ticket.

It should be noted that these were all "ticket" cases, where a ticket was purchased but no waiver document signed. The principles developed in these rulings continue to be applicable today — especially in cases such as ski-hill accidents, where tickets have been purchased. Most cases usually revolve around the question of notice to the customer. Cases that include the signing of a waiver are similar. In fact, the signature collected on a waiver proves a greater level of notice and it is assumed that an adult signing a document reads its contents.

A relatively modern "ticket" case in Canada is the British Columbia case of *Union Steamships Ltd. v. Barnes*, (13) a judgement of the Supreme Court of Canada in 1956. In a suit by a passenger who had come on board at Toba Inlet bound for Vancouver and who, soon after boarding the ship, fell down a dark passageway and suffered injuries, the steamship company successfully relied on an exemption clause.

A leading English case on signed waivers in the modern era is the 1934 case of *L'Estrange v. Graucob*. (14) There, the Divisional Court adopted and applied the principle of notice laid down in 1877 by the Parker case referred to earlier. The case of L'Estrange has been often cited and applied by Canadian courts in recent times. Examples from Canadian courts include *Delaney v. Cascade River Holidays Ltd.*, (15) the case of a fatal accident arising from a whitewater rafting trip on the Fraser River; and *Karroll v. Silver Star Mountain Resorts Ltd.*, (16) a case resulting from a ski accident at Silver Star Mountain during a ski race. The Manitoba courts dealt with the same sort of issue in the context of injuries arising from a snowmobile accident that occurred during a race. The appeal of the case, *Dyck v. Manitoba Snowmobile Association Inc. and Wood*, (17) to the Supreme Court of Canada largely revolved on the question of whether it was unconscionable to uphold the waiver. The Court found that it was not, and the case was dismissed. (18) In all of these examples, the defense of waiver prevailed.

More recent examples of upheld waiver cases include *Ocsko v. Cypress Bowl Recreations Ltd.*; (19) *Shuster v. Blackcomb Skiing Enterprises Ltd.*, (20) a case arising from a skiing accident at Blackcomb Mountain where a waiver was signed prior to participation in the "Ski Esprit" program; *Knowles v. Whistler Mountain Ski Corporation*, (21) where a waiver was signed when ski equipment was rented; *Ochoa v. Canadian Mountain Holidays Inc. et al.*, (22) where a waiver was signed before a heli-skiing trip; and *Mayer v. Big White Ski Resort Ltd.*, (23) where a waiver was signed during the purchase of a season's pass.

The Principle of Notice

One of the dominant questions regarding the validity of exclusionary clauses in tickets and waivers is that of adequate notice, i.e. did the party seeking its protection bring the contract sufficiently to the notice of the other party? In the case of *Karroll v. Silver Star Mountain Resorts Ltd.*, Chief Justice of the Supreme Court McLachlin said in her judgement at Page 167:

> Were the circumstances of the signing such that a reasonable person should have known that Miss Karroll did not intend to agree to what she signed? I think not. First, the release was consistent with the purpose of the contract. As in *Delaney v. Cascade River Holidays Ltd.*, the purpose of the contract was to permit Miss Karroll to engage in a hazardous activity upon which she, of her own volition, desired to embark. The exclusion of legal liability was consistent with the purpose of permitting her and others to engage in this activity, while limiting the liability of the organizations which made the activity possible.
>
> Second, the release was short, easy to read and headed in capital letters "RELEASE AND INDEMNITY — PLEASE READ CAREFULLY." The most casual glance would reveal to a reasonable person that this was a legal document calculated to release those staging the race from liability. There was no fine print. The printing was entirely contained by the page signed. This was not a case of a release buried in the fine print of a long document, but of a release that proclaimed its purpose in bold letters. In sum, the nature of the document does not give rise to the suggestion that a person signing would not be in agreement with its terms.
>
> Third, it emerges from the evidence that signing such waivers was a common feature of this ski race. Miss Karroll herself had signed such waivers on previous

occasions before similar races. This was not an unusual term; on the contrary, it was a standard aspect of this type of contract.

These facts negate the inference that a reasonable person in the defendant Silver Star's position would conclude that Miss Karroll was not agreeing to the terms of the release. In these circumstances, it was not incumbent on Silver Star to take reasonable steps to bring the contents of the release to her attention or ensure that she read it fully.

If I were wrong in this conclusion, I would nevertheless find that Silver Star took reasonable steps to discharge any obligation to bring the contents of the release to the attention of Miss Karroll. I have already referred to the heading at the top of the document, and the capitalized admonition to read it carefully. This was sufficient to bring the need to read the document to the attention of a reasonable person. Miss Karroll admitted that she could have read the release in one to two minutes. She further admitted that she could not recall if she had an opportunity to take one or two minutes to read through the document. Thus the evidence fails to establish that she was not given sufficient time to peruse the document had she wished to do so.

Regarding the issue of whether or not an operator is required to provide verbal notice of what is contained in the waiver, in the earlier case of *Union Steamships Ltd. v. Barnes*, Justice Locke, giving the judgement of the Court, stated the following at Page 545:

In *Hood v. Anchor Line (Henderson Bros.) Ltd.*, (24) Viscount Haldane reiterated what he had said in the Robinson case, that the question as to whether what was reasonably necessary to be done to draw the passenger's attention to the terms of the contract was, in substance, one of fact. Lord Finlay L.C., referring to the Parker case, said that it showed that (p. 842): "If it is found that the company did what was reasonably sufficient to give notice of conditions printed on the back of a ticket the person taking the ticket would be bound by such conditions." Lord Parmoor, after saying that the Lord Ordinary had found that the respondent had done what was reasonably sufficient to give the appellant notice of the conditions, said that it was not material that other or different steps might have been taken, and that a clearly printed notice on the envelope which enclosed the ticket and on the face of the ticket was as effective for this purpose as if the representative of the respondents had, at the time when he issued the ticket, verbally called the attention of the appellant to the conditions and asked him to read them.

When There Is a Lack of Notice
Irrespective of the rulings listed above, which are consistently in favour of the defendant, there is one recent ticket case where the court ruled that inadequate notice was provided to the plaintiff and that the waiver did not hold.

In a decision of the Chief Justice in the case of *Greeven v. Blackcomb Skiing Enterprises*

Ltd., (25) Blackcomb Skiing Enterprises Ltd. failed on a waiver defense because it was unable to demonstrate that due notice of a waiver or a limitation of liability had been brought home to the plaintiff, Greeven. There was unsatisfactory evidence as to the nature of signage at the area of the ticket booth where the plaintiff purchased her ticket, and, as well, it was established that the plaintiff had never been at the ski area before and was not at all aware of the situation. At Page 6 of the reasons, the Chief Justice said the following in support of the plaintiff:

> In this case, the plaintiff, Greeven, was a stranger to the country and to the mountain and purchased the ticket at the very beginning of her visit. Counsel for the plaintiff says there is no case to be found in which a plaintiff innocent of any degree of knowledge of the writing has been held to be bound. That may be so, but neither the cases nor section 4(1) of the act require actual notice if the defendant establishes that it has taken reasonable steps to bring the terms to the attention of the customer.
>
> In this case, I find that the defendant has not discharged that burden in relation to this plaintiff. The notices are garish, and are reasonably legible and clear in their wording. But the evidence as to their location in relation to the ticket wickets, as to their number and as to the other circumstances existing on that day is vague. I cannot conclude that the plaintiff should have seen any of them. There is nothing about the tickets themselves that would necessarily draw to the attention of a reasonably alert person without prior knowledge that they contain writing other than the advertising and definition of the period for which they are issued.

Unconscionability of Waivers

A number of plaintiffs have argued that waiver contracts are unconscionable because they are "so manifestly unfair and unreasonable [as] to be unenforceable". (26) The argument here is that the waiver clause "diverges sufficiently from community standards of commercial morality that it should be unenforceable as unfair and unreasonable". (27)

In *Hunter Engineering Co. v. Syncrude Canada Ltd.*, (28) Madam Justice Wilson concluded that contracts should be enforced unless unconscionable, saying at Page 461: "There appears to be no sound reason for applying special rules in the case of clauses excluding liability than for other clauses producing harsh results," and at Page 462: "Only where the contract is unconscionable, as might arise from situations of unequal bargaining power between the parties, should the courts interfere with agreements the parties have freely concluded. The courts do not blindly enforce harsh or unconscionable bargains...." Since tourism guests have the ability to not agree to the waiver terms, they are not in an "unequal bargaining position" — even though the effect of an enforced waiver might seem "harsh" at the time.

In *Harry v. Kreutziger*, (29) Justice Lambert stated: "The single question in cases where enforceability of a contract comes to be decided is whether the transaction, seen as a whole, is sufficiently divergent from community standards of commercial morality that it should be rescinded." Strongly worded contract terms exist in all forms of business transactions, and those found in a waiver are consistent with business standards — both within and without the adventure industry.

In *Knowles v. Whistler Mountain Ski Corporation*, Madam Justice Huddart, ruling in favour of Whistler Mountain during a ski-rental suit, stated:

> The plaintiffs argue that the release agreement constitutes an unconscionable bargain for several reasons. It is a standard form contract, one-sided in favor of the party who drafted it. There was no opportunity for negotiations. The parties were in unequal bargaining positions. The clause is unusual because it seeks to exclude all liability. The procedures involved in executing the contract suggest to the ski renter that the shop was taking care to adjust the bindings properly, thereby leading the ordinary renter to believe that the exclusion clause would not apply to negligence relating to the bindings adjustment. Their counsel ... says that if renters were aware they were releasing claims founded on incompetence and that those procedures were a sham, no one would ski.
>
> I disagree. I cannot see anything in the nature of the Release Agreement or in the circumstances in which it was signed divergent from community standards of commercial activity.
>
> There is no evidence of duress, coercion, or unfair advantage, resulting from economic or psychological need or the inability to understand the nature of the contract. Nothing that was said or done could have led anyone to believe the waiver would not apply.

Reading the Waiver before Signing It

The courts have ruled that it may be immaterial whether or not the customer read the waiver document and was aware of its contents, i.e. whether or not the plaintiff appreciated that he or she was signing a document that affected his or her legal rights.

For example, in *Karroll v. Silver Star Mountain Resorts Ltd.*, Madam Justice McLachlin stated at Page 164:

> One must begin from the proposition set out in *L'Estrange v. F. Graucob Ltd.* at pages 406–407, that "where a party has signed a written agreement it is immaterial to the question of his liability under it that he has not read its contents." Maugham L.J. went on to state two exceptions to this rule.
>
> The first is where the document is signed by the plaintiff "in circumstances which made it not her act" (*non est factum*). The second is where the agreement has been induced by fraud or misrepresentation.
>
> To these exceptions a third has been added. Where the party seeking to enforce the document knew or had reason to know of the other's mistake as to its terms, those

terms should not be enforced. This new exception is entirely in the spirit of the two recognized in 1934 in *L'Estrange v. F. Graucob Ltd.* Where a party has reason to believe that the signing party is mistaken as to a term, then the signing party cannot reasonably have been taken to have consented to that term, with the result that the signature which purportedly binds him to it is not his consensual act. Similarly, to allow someone to believe he is mistaken as to its contents is not far distant from active misrepresentation.

In the usual commercial situation, there is no need for the party presenting the document to bring exclusions of liability or onerous terms to the attention of the signing party, nor need he advise him to read the document. In such situations, it is safe to assume that the party signing the contract intends to be bound by its terms.

This last exception is often called "the third exception" and is an important concept to understand. Although a signed contract is legally binding, in the case of a guest who does not seem to know what he or she is signing it is far better to bring it to his or her attention rather than misrepresent what is contained in the document.

In *Mayer v. Big White Ski Resort Ltd.*, Justice Bauman stated in his judgement:

While this plaintiff does not plead *non est factum*, his carelessness in signing the Release should certainly preclude the successful invocation of that defense. Here the plaintiff expressly questioned the nature of the document. He had it in his possession on two occasions, first when he signed it and then when he printed his name and address at the top of the document. He chose not to read the document. He had ample opportunity to do so. He cannot now complain that he did not understand the nature of the Release.

Translating Waivers to Foreign Clients

In recent years, the access of adventure operators to ever-increasing foreign markets has raised the question of how businesses should present waivers to non-English-speaking clients. While most operators have made no changes to their waivers and continue to present English-only documents to their foreign clients, other companies have made attempts to translate their documents or to have a translator present. A business must be able to prove that the guest knew and understood the release, and it should make every effort to provide a waiver in the guest's first language.

The one, often-quoted, case exception to the above is *Ochoa v. Canadian Mountain Holidays Inc. et al.*, where an English waiver was upheld when signed by a non-English-speaking client from Mexico. Madam Justice Koenigsberg stated in her judgement:

Considering the facts in this case and applying the principles of law which are outlined above, there can be no finding that Mr. Ochoa is not bound by the waiver he signed on

December 10, 1990 on the basis that he did not know what he was signing. He knew or had every reason to know that the document affected his legal rights. He was aware of the risks involved in participating in the sport of heli-skiing, and he had every opportunity to read (by translation) the waiver, but he declined to do so. In the circumstances the only reasonable conclusion to be drawn from Mr. Ochoa's witnessed signature is that the actual contents of the waiver were immaterial to him. He was prepared to be bound by the contract.

The reason that care must be taken in drawing generalizations from the above statement is that Mr. Ochoa carried out a significant amount of business in international circles and had a personal assistant who acted as his English interpreter in day-to-day business affairs. In addition, he had an English-speaking wife. Someone else in other circumstances might be viewed differently.

Witnessing the Waiver

The question of whether a waiver should be witnessed — and by whom — is often faced by operators. Although I have not found a great deal of information regarding this directly from court rulings, in the case of *Mayer v. Big White Ski Resort Ltd.*, Justice Bauman stated in his judgement:

> I should touch on one further matter. The evidence before me indicated that an employee of the corporate defendant did not initially fill in the witness box on the Release. Apparently, on the day of the accident, an employee of the corporate defendant, on retrieving the Release, saw that the witness had not signed and took it upon himself, without the knowledge of the corporate defendant, to complete the witness box. This is obviously improper but I do not believe that it undermines the essential validity of the document. There is no doubt that the plaintiff executed the Release. I conclude that the Release is binding and enforceable.

In the event that a signed waiver is brought to court, there will be a need to prove that the signature is that of the plaintiff. The best way of doing this is for the business to establish a consistent waiver-signing and -collection process. Guest signatures can be witnessed by business employees.

Waivers and Negligence

Criminal, or Gross, Negligence

Criminal, or gross, negligence may be defined as wanton or reckless disregard for the life or safety of another person. Waiver documents do not cover criminal negligence; however, they are usually written in such a manner as to cover negligence, with the inclusion of a *negligence clause*. In order to establish criminal negligence, one must first determine negligence. Commenting on criminal negligence in *Ochoa v. Canadian Mountain Holidays Inc. et al.*, Madam Justice Koenigsberg stated in her judgement:

> The acts or omissions complained of must depart from a reasonable standard. Second, the acts or omissions must be more than a departure from a reasonable standard. There must be a marked departure in all the circumstances of the case. Third, having found a marked departure from the standards of reasonableness, one must be able to infer on an objective foresight test that the defendant failed to direct his or her mind to the risk and the need to take care. However, the essential element which illuminates the concept of marked departure is that of recklessness. At Page 679 of the Creighton decision, the *actus reus* is described as follows:
>
> > This may consist in carrying out the activity in a dangerous fashion, or in embarking on the activity when in all the circumstances it is dangerous to do so.

Negligence

Negligence can be defined as an error in judgement or skill, or both, which falls below a reasonable standard of care in a specific industry. As stated by Fridman in Volume 1 of *The Law of Torts* (1986) at Page 289: "Liability in tort will only arise where a defendant has transgressed the standards to be expected of a reasonable man, not where he has acted with due care but nevertheless made what turned out to be a wrong decision." (*See also Chapter Two.*)

In *Lowry v. Canadian Mountain Holidays Ltd.*, (30) dealing with an avalanche accident, the Court of Appeal, in setting a standard for negligent conduct in the heli-ski industry, asked at Page 11: "Did the defendant exercise reasonable care in the circumstances?" In *Scurfield v. Cariboo Helicopter Skiing Ltd.*, (31) another case dealing with an avalanche accident in a heli-ski operation, the Court said at Page 225:

> It is not contended that the defendants had a duty to ensure that their guests were kept away from all places where avalanches could occur. In the context of helicopter skiing that would be impossible. I think it correct to say the duty of care which lay on the defendants was not to expose their guests to risks regarded in the business as unreasonably high, whether from avalanche or any other hazard to which participants in the sport are normally exposed. To enjoy the excitement of skiing in mountain wilderness areas participants are necessarily exposed both to risks which the careful skier is able to avoid and certain risks also which such skiers may be unable to avoid, including some risk of being caught in an inescapable avalanche.

In *Ochoa v. Canadian Mountain Holidays Inc. et al.*, Madam Justice Koenigsberg stated in her judgement:

There can be no doubt that the determination of what constitutes an unreasonably high risk must be in the eyes of a reasonably competent heli-ski guide. And perhaps most importantly, the approach as to what constitutes a reasonable or unreasonable risk in any given circumstance from the point of view of a reasonably competent heli-ski guide must not be ascertained in hindsight. As to the importance of this approach, L'Heureux-Dube in *LaPointe v. Hospital Le Gardeur*, (32) at page 90, said:

> As a general rule, the obligation of a physician and a hospital toward a patient is not one of result but of means, that is an obligation of prudence and diligence whose violation is not to be assessed subjectively by inquiring whether the author of an act or omission has done his best, but rather according to an objective and abstract criterion under which the court asks what another doctor, another specialist ... of ordinary and reasonable knowledge, competence and skill would have done in circumstances similar to those in which the person whose conduct is to be judged found himself or herself...
>
> ...courts should be careful not to rely upon the perfect vision afforded by hindsight. In order to evaluate a particular exercise of judgement fairly, the doctor's limited ability to foresee future events when determining a course of conduct must be borne in mind.
>
> Otherwise the doctor will not be assessed according to the norms of the average doctor of reasonable ability in the same circumstances but rather will be held accountable for mistakes that are apparent only after the fact...

In attempting to prove negligence against a guide or operator, the plaintiff's case depends on the court making one or more of the following findings:

❖ The decision to carry out the activity was a decision based on negligent application of the skill and knowledge of reasonably competent guides in the same activity.

❖ The guide in charge when the accident occurred failed to exercise the skill and care of a reasonably competent guide.

❖ The system for risk assessment was below the standard in the profession.

❖ The industry standards for the activity are negligent.

Application of Waivers

Ultimately, a court decision on the validity of a waiver will rest on the question of whether or not the waiver used covers negligence of the kind alleged in the suit. (33) Any waiver seeking to cover negligent conduct must contain something more than the term "negligence". That something more includes, at the least, a context describing the kind of conduct amounting to negligence which is intended to be covered; the court must be satisfied that the individual signing the waiver, if he or she read the document, could reasonably be expected to understand the term's meaning.

Madam Justice Koenigsberg's ruling on *Ochoa v. Canadian Mountain Holidays Inc. et al.* at Page 75 covers several of the issues surrounding the application of waivers:

> I hasten to add that the authorities on this subject do not require that that understanding be objectively found on the waiver alone. It may be gleaned from the circumstances of the individual's knowledge of the activity at issue coupled with the document under consideration. On that basis, I find that the waiver in this case, signed by Mr. Ochoa, meets that test.
>
> First, the waiver format and substance, if read carefully, can reasonably be understood to include a waiver of liability for negligence or a want of due care of CMH and its staff in its conduct, particularly in relation to assessing avalanche hazard. Such a risk is dealt with specifically and generally as a risk contemplated by the waiver.
>
> Second, the format of the waiver is not at all deceptive or difficult to read. While some of the print is small, it puts in bold letters several attention-getting words of warning that legal rights are at issue.
>
> Finally, CMH takes several steps to ensure that each of its guests is aware, well in advance of the trip, of the requirement to sign a waiver as a condition of heli-skiing with CMH and that CMH considers the document important. These steps include requiring that the signature for the waiver be witnessed separately from the application form that accompanied it. These steps add to the conclusion that the meaning of the waiver is neither obscure nor unreasonable. The very type of conduct alleged to be negligent in this action is specifically contemplated by the words of the waiver. I have no hesitation in finding that the negligence alleged in this action is covered by the waiver.

Waiver Controversy

There is much controversy and misunderstanding on the part of both operators and customers around the use of waivers. Some of the relevant issues are clearly articulated in the Law Reform Commission of British Columbia's 1994 *Report on Recreational Injuries: Liability and Waivers in Commercial Leisure Activities*, on Page 33:

> It is nothing new for users to be required to sign a comprehensive waiver to obtain membership in a sports organisation, as part of an application for a pass enabling regular use of a recreational facility or an entry form for competitions, nor is it unusual to encounter waiver terms on admission tickets. The breadth of some waivers now in use is nevertheless controversial.
>
> Increased explicitness in the wording and format of more sophisticated waivers, together with a higher rate of participation in sports that were formerly engaged in only by the more adventurous, is partly responsible for the controversy. A few recent decisions upholding recreational waivers have attracted a degree of publicity, bringing

public misconceptions about them into collision with the legal reality.

A misconception that emerged repeatedly in the responses to the Consultation Paper, as well as in informal consultation, is that waivers are "not worth the paper they are printed on." This mistaken belief is held not only by members of the general public, but even among some commercial operators and recreational organisations. It probably stems from a misunderstanding of "ticket cases" in which unsigned exclusionary terms were not enforced because the consumer's attention was not adequately drawn to them. It was common in the past to print exclusionary terms on the back of tickets in virtually unreadable print, and examples of this practice are still found.

Similarly, it is often thought that waivers are intended to protect the operator and its employees only against liability for fortuitous accidents, not against their own negligence. The reference to the operator's own negligence is sometimes buried in the middle of a lengthy paragraph, for obviously disingenuous reasons.

Another misconception is that waivers cannot afford protection in the event of "gross negligence," which is true in some jurisdictions but not in British Columbia, apart from instances where liability is governed by specific legislative provisions that distinguish between degrees of negligence.

Without waivers, operators and their insurers believe they lose control over their exposure to liability. Negligence law is based on judicial decisions that are highly dependent on individual fact patterns. They do not provide operators with a coherent body of practical rules that, if followed, will avoid entanglement in personal injury litigation. The cost of defending all personal injury claims, even those that are dismissed, consumes premium revenue and impairs the ability of insurers to create reserves to meet real liabilities.

Despite the importance attached by industry to waivers, and the increased use of explicit language, it is still easy to find waivers and ticket terms in use that are written in complex, legalistic "boilerplate" that most users will not read or take the time to try to understand, although their lives may be drastically affected by it.

Law Reform and the Future of Waivers

There is little doubt that waivers provide a useful service to adventure operators and insurers by discouraging claims and protecting operators in the case of a legal suit. Arguments can be made both for and against comprehensive waivers; however, the more attention they receive and the more policy makers and the public understand their use, the greater the potential for a backlash against them. For a good example of this mode of thought, consider the position of the Law Reform Commission of British Columbia, again in its 1994 *Report on Recreational Injuries: Liability and Waivers in Commercial Leisure Activities*, which states on Page 46:

The effect of comprehensive waivers in recreation reaches beyond that of a risk-allocating arrangement under a private business transaction. Where an injury is negligently inflicted, the effect of a comprehensive waiver is to transfer the associated costs to society. In the case of serious or catastrophic injury, the cost of initial treatment, rehabilitation, continuing care, and temporary or permanent loss of the victim's productive capacity, is a significant burden. The present value of the cost of lifetime care for a quadriplegic, for example, generally exceeds $1,000,000. When liability is present, the loss is likely to be met from insurance funded from the operator's gross revenues, and therefore ultimately by users. In this way, the risk is spread across the user population, but not across society at large.

At the time of this report, the Law Reform Commission's mandate was "to take and keep under review all the law of the Province, including statute law, common law and judicial decisions, with a view to its systematic development and reform". (34) In its report, the Commission made the following recommendations specifically regarding the future use of waivers. (35) They are provided here as an indication of the types of arguments presented against waivers.

✦ A commercial recreational operator should not be able to exclude or limit its liability for personal injury or death arising from:
   a) malfunction of equipment under the control of the operator;
   b) unsafe operation of mechanical equipment;
   c) unsafe aspects of the structure and condition of an indoor recreation facility;
   d) failure by the operator of an outdoor recreational facility to maintain commonly accepted conditions of demarcation, signage, lighting and monitoring;
   e) unfitness for normal use, at the time of supply or rental, of equipment;
   f) conduct of the operator's employees, acting in the course of their employment, that results in personal injury to or death of a user from the sources of risk referred to in (a) to (e); or
   g) breach by the operator, or by an employee of the operator, of a statutory duty or regulatory requirement.

✦ A recreational operator should remain able to limit or exclude its liability to adult users for personal injury, death, or damage to property, stemming from risks associated with a recreational activity itself.

✦ An operator should not be able to make participation in a recreational activity conditional on terms that exclude liability for injury or loss arising from anything other than the recreational activity.

✦ Any exclusionary terms protecting an operator from claims for injury or loss arising from anything other than that connected to the recreational activity itself should be the subject of a separate agreement and should not be contained in the same document.

❖ The practice of requiring a minor or the minor's parent or guardian to agree to terms excluding liability for personal injury to the minor should be prohibited. Such an agreement, if obtained, should be unenforceable.

❖ It should be permissible to obtain from a minor, or from the minor's parents or guardians, a signed acknowledgement that a recreational activity involves inherent risks, and that the minor assumes them in order to be permitted to engage in the activity.

❖ The liability of an operator towards an adult user should be limited to the percentage share of fault apportioned to the operator.

❖ A non-profit recreational organization and its members should be expressly permitted to exclude its liability to an adult member for personal injury or death arising from the adult member's participation in the activities of the organization.

❖ When a non-profit recreational organization offers a recreational opportunity on a profit-seeking basis to the general public as well as to its own members, its ability to exclude its liability for personal injury or death towards adult non-members should be equivalent to that of a commercial operator.

Indemnifications

Most waivers include an indemnification. A waiver intended to be signed by an adult on his or her own behalf might include a statement such as: "I agree to hold harmless and indemnify the company from any and all liability for any property damage, or personal injury to any third party, resulting from my participation in [wilderness skiing]."

To indemnify means to make compensation to the business (i.e. pay it back). Broadly worded, an indemnification clause may be applied to costs such as those paid out by the business for damage to property or to other participants caused by the person signing the waiver, or for rescue and evacuation relating to that person.

Indemnifications Signed by Parents on Behalf of Minors

A waiver signed by a minor is unenforceable under the *Infant Act* in many jurisdictions. It is therefore common for a business to have a parent sign an indemnification for costs it might incur while taking the parent's child (presumably a minor) on a program. An indemnification is an attempt to indirectly prevent a lawsuit by a minor by inserting a term (or using a completely separate indemnification agreement) whereby the parent agrees to indemnify the operator for any liability the operator may have towards the minor. If the parent sues on behalf of the minor and the operator is compelled to pay damages, the parent would theoretically be bound contractually to reimburse the operator. In this way, the parent is discouraged from suing on the minor's behalf. Such an indemnification might read something like this:

> I agree that my son or daughter, being an infant, will be participating in [program] and that those infants or minors may not be contractually bound by a Release of All Claims and Waiver of Liability Agreement which I have seen and I have signed. I therefore specifically agree to indemnify [company] against any and all claims, actions, and suits that may be instituted by my son or daughter.

This type of indemnity clause is contained in waivers used by many camps and sports instruction programs for children across North America. However, its enforceability is uncertain in Canada. The use of such statements, while legal at the moment, has been under law-reviewer scrutiny for some time. For example, the following was one of the recommendations in the B.C. Law Reform Commission's 1994 *Report on Recreational Injuries: Liability and Waivers in Commercial Leisure Activities*: "An agreement whereby a parent or guardian of a minor agrees to indemnify a person in respect of any legal action brought on behalf of the minor should be prohibited. Such an agreement, if obtained, should be unenforceable." In Ontario, an indemnity of this type has been held to be unenforceable. (36)

Therefore, although the case law regarding minors and indemnifications remains unclear, "[it is] likely that a court would rule that by using an indemnification the business was attempting to achieve indirectly what they could not achieve directly — and rule that this continued to be against the minor's interest, and thus against public policy." (37)

Appendix 6–1 — Sample Waiver Form

SUSHI GREEN ADVENTURE TOURS LTD. (38)
RELEASE OF LIABILITY, WAIVER OF CLAIMS,
ASSUMPTION OF RISK AND INDEMNITY AGREEMENT

AVALANCHE COURSES OFFERED BY SUSHI GREEN ADVENTURE TOURS LTD. ARE OFTEN CONDUCTED IN HAZARDOUS MOUNTAIN TERRAIN. THESE COURSES INVOLVE RISKS, DANGERS AND HAZARDS IN ADDITION TO THOSE NORMALLY ASSOCIATED WITH BEING IN A MOUNTAIN ENVIRONMENT. ALL COURSE PARTICIPANTS ARE REQUIRED TO SIGN THIS RELEASE OF LIABILITY AND WAIVER AGREEMENT. BY SIGNING THIS AGREEMENT YOU WILL WAIVE OR GIVE UP CERTAIN LEGAL RIGHTS, INCLUDING THE RIGHT TO SUE SHOULD YOU BE INJURED. PLEASE READ CAREFULLY!

TO: SUSHI GREEN ADVENTURE TOURS LTD. (hereinafter referred to as "THE COMPANY")

Name _____   Name of Course _____

Address _____   Date of Course _____

DEFINITIONS:
In this agreement:

The term "MOUNTAIN TRAVEL" shall include, but is not limited to: skiing; snowboarding; snowshoeing; hiking and climbing; and all travel by snowmobile, snowcat, motor vehicle, aircraft and other conveyances.

The term "AVALANCHE COURSE" shall include all courses, seminars, workshops, activities, services and use of facilities in any way related to the course I have registered for, as outlined in THE COMPANY'S brochure including, but not limited to: classroom sessions; field trips; all mountain travel either within or beyond ski-area boundaries or in the backcountry; and all transportation by air or on public or private roads or highways in connection with the course.

ASSUMPTION OF RISKS — AVALANCHES, MOUNTAIN TRAVEL, WEATHER, ETC.
I am aware that the course I have registered for takes place in hazardous mountainous terrain and involves various risks, dangers and hazards. Avalanches occur frequently in the mountain terrain in which the Avalanche Course is conducted. I acknowledge and accept

that the Avalanche Course instructors may fail to predict whether the mountain terrain is safe for travel or whether avalanches may occur. The mountain terrain in which the avalanche course is taught is uncontrolled, unmarked, not inspected and involves many risks, dangers and hazards in addition to that of avalanches. These may include but are not limited to: ice and snow cornices; trees, tree wells and tree stumps; creeks; rocks and boulders; forest deadfall; holes and depressions on or beneath the snow surface; cliffs; variable and difficult snow conditions; crevasses; winter travel on highways and backcountry roads; snowcat roads and road banks, fences and other man-made structures; becoming lost or separated from the Avalanche Course instructor or other course participants; extreme and rapidly changing weather conditions; negligence of other persons; mechanical failure of snowmobiles, snowcats and related equipment; impact or collision with other persons or snowmobiles, snowcats and other vehicles; failure to operate a snowmobile safely or within one's own ability; AND NEGLIGENCE ON THE PART OF THE RELEASEES, INCLUDING THE FAILURE BY THE RELEASEES TO SAFEGUARD OR PROTECT ME FROM THE RISKS, DANGERS AND HAZARDS REFERRED TO ABOVE.

I AM AWARE OF THE RISKS, DANGERS AND HAZARDS ASSOCIATED WITH PARTICIPATING IN THE AVALANCHE COURSE AND I FREELY ACCEPT AND FULLY ASSUME ALL SUCH RISKS, DANGERS AND HAZARDS AND THE POSSIBILITY OF PERSONAL INJURY, DEATH, PROPERTY DAMAGE OR LOSS RESULTING THEREFROM.

NOTICE TO COURSE PARTICIPANTS USING SNOWBOARDS, SNOWSHOES AND TELEMARK SKIS — INCREASED RISK
Unlike alpine ski boot/binding systems, snowboard, snowshoe and some telemark boot/binding systems are not designed or intended to release and will not release under normal circumstances. The use of a safety strap or retention device by snowboarders or telemark skiers who do not have ski brakes will increase the risk of not surviving an avalanche.

RELEASE OF LIABILITY, WAIVER OF CLAIMS AND INDEMNITY AGREEMENT
In consideration of being permitted to participate in the Avalanche Course, and for other good and valuable consideration, the receipt and sufficiency of which is acknowledged, I hereby agree as follows:

To WAIVE ANY AND ALL CLAIMS that I have or may in the future have against the Releasees arising out of any aspect of my participation in the avalanche course;
TO RELEASE THE RELEASEES from any and all liability for any loss, damage, expense or injury including death that I may suffer or that my next of kin my suffer during my

participation in the avalanche course, DUE TO ANY CAUSE WHATSOEVER, INCLUD-
ING NEGLIGENCE, BREACH OF CONTRACT, OR BREACH OF ANY STATUTORY
OR OTHER DUTY OF CARE, AS WELL AS ANY DUTY OF CARE OWED UNDER
THE OCCUPIERS LIABILITY ACT R.S.B.C C. 1996, c. 337, ON THE PART OF THE
RELEASEES, AND ALSO INCLUDING THE FAILURE ON THE PART OF
THE RELEASEES TO SAFEGUARD OR PROTECT ME FROM THE RISKS, DANGERS
AND HAZARDS OF THE AVALANCHE COURSE REFERRED TO ABOVE. TO HOLD
HARMLESS AND INDEMNIFY THE RELEASEES from any and all liability for any prop-
erty damage or personal injury to any third party resulting from my participation in the
Avalanche Course;

    This Agreement shall be effective and binding upon my heirs, next of kin, executors,
administrators, assigns and representatives, in the event of my death or incapacity;

    This Agreement shall be governed by and interpreted in accordance with the laws of
the Province of British Columbia; and

    Any litigation involving the parties to this Agreement shall be brought within the
Province of British Columbia.

In entering into this Agreement, I am not relying on any oral or written representation or
statements made by the Releasees with respect to the safety of the Avalanche Course, other
than what is set forth in this Agreement.

I CONFIRM THAT I HAVE READ AND UNDERSTOOD THIS AGREEMENT PRIOR TO
SIGNING IT, AND I AM AWARE THAT BY SIGNING THIS AGREEMENT I AM WAIV-
ING CERTAIN LEGAL RIGHTS WHICH I OR MY HEIRS, NEXT OF KIN, EXECUTORS,
ADMINISTRATORS, ASSIGNS AND REPRESENTATIVES MAY HAVE AGAINST THE
RELEASEES.

Signed this _____ day of _____ 20___ at _____

Signature of Participant _____

Please print name clearly _____

Signature of Witness _____

Please print name clearly _____

Appendix 6–2 — Sample Indemnification Form

SUSHI GREEN ADVENTURE TOURS LTD.
INDEMNITY AGREEMENT

WARNING: IF A LAWSUIT IS BROUGHT AGAINST SUSHI GREEN ADVENTURE TOURS LTD., ITS OFFICERS, EMPLOYEES, AGENTS, REPRESENTATIVES AND INDEPENDENT CONTRACTORS (HEREINAFTER COLLECTIVELY CALLED THE "COMPANY"), THEN THE COMPANY HAS THE RIGHT TO INDEMNIFY AGAINST ME.

TO: SUSHI GREEN ADVENTURE TOURS LTD.

I agree that my son or daughter, being an infant, will be participating in an Avalanche Course (hereinafter referred to as "the Course") and that this infant or minor may not be contractually bound by a Release of All Claims, Waiver of Liability and Assumption of Risk Agreement which I have seen and I have signed. I therefore specifically agree to indemnify the Company against any and all claims, actions and suits that may be instituted by my son or daughter.

I AGREE TO SAVE HARMLESS AND INDEMNIFY THE COMPANY from any cause of action, suit, claim or liability of any kind whatsoever arising out of any cause whatsoever but not limited to negligence on the part of the Company.

In entering into this Agreement, I am not relying on any oral or written representations or statements made by the Company including those in any brochure issued by the Company, to induce me or my son or daughter to undertake and to participate in the activity.

I confirm that I have read and understood this Indemnity Agreement prior to signing it, and agree that this Agreement will be binding upon me, my heirs, next of kin, executors, administrators and assigns.

I agree that this Agreement is to be interpreted according to the laws of the Province of British Columbia and I understand that if I have any questions regarding the waiver of my rights, or this Indemnity Agreement, I should consult a lawyer prior to signing this Agreement.

Signed this _____ day of _____ 20___ at _____

Signature of Participant _____ Please print name clearly _____

Signature of Witness _____ Please print name clearly _____

Notes to Chapter Six

1. Law Reform Commission of British Columbia, *Report on Recreational Injuries: Liability and waivers in Commercial Leisure Activities*, 1994.

2. See, among others: *Karroll v. Silver Star Mountain Resorts Ltd.* (1988), 33 B.C.L.R. (2d) 160 (S.C.); *Scurfield v. Cariboo Helicopter Skiing Ltd.* (June 8, 1990), Vancouver A861515 (B.C.S.C.), reversed, [1993] 3 W.W.R. (C.A.); *Knowles v. Whistler Mountain Ski Corporation et al.* (December 11, 1990), Vancouver C900215 (B.C.S.C.); *Ocsko v. Cypress Bowl Recreations Ltd.* (1992), 74 B.C.L.R. (2d) 159 (C.A.); *Blomberg v. Blackcomb Skiing Enterprises Ltd.* (1992), 74 B.C.L.R. (2d) 51 (S.C.); *McQuary v. Big White Ski Resort Ltd.* (October 4, 1993), Victoria 90-1214 (B.C.S.C.); *Dawe v. Cypress Bowl Recreations Ltd.* (November 24, 1993), Nanaimo 01933 (B.C.S.C.); *Greeven v. Blackcomb Skiing Enterprises Ltd.* (September 19, 1994), Vancouver C927644 (B.C.S.C.); *Shuster v. Blackcomb Skiing Enterprises Ltd.* (November 21, 1994), Vancouver C934644 (B.C.S.C.); and *Ochoa v. Canadian Mountain Holidays Inc.* (September 25, 1996), Vancouver C922041 (B.C.S.C.).

3. Adapted from Lord Justice Maugham, in *L'Estrange v. F. Graucob*, [1934] 2 K.B. 394.

4. From: M. Blaxland, C. Macmillan and R. Kennedy, "Guidelines for Obtaining Waivers from Participants", *Continuing Legal Education* (April, 1989).

5. Ibid.

6. *Infants Act*, R.S.B.C. C. 1979, c. 196, s. 16.2. There is provision in ss. 16.4 and 16.5 of the Act for the court or the Public Trustee to grant capacity to minors to enter into binding contracts, but only in respect of contracts that are clearly for their benefit. Contracts made by minors have also been held to be unenforceable in common law, except in a few exceptional cases.

7. S. 31(1) of the *Infants Act*, ibid., allows a guardian (which, under s. 27 of the *Family Relations Act*, R.S.B.C. 1979, c. 121, includes a parent) to make a binding agreement for a minor only with the approval of the court. The Public Trustee may approve the agreement if the consideration is $10,000 or less.

8. Law Reform Commission of British Columbia, *Report on Recreational Injuries: Liability and Waivers in Commercial Leisure Activities*, 1994.

9. (1862), 31 L.J.C.P. (N.S.) 241.

10. (1876), 1 Q.B.D. 515.

11. (1877), 2 C.P.D. 416.

12. [1918] A.C. 837.

13. (1956), 5 D.L.R. (2d) 535.

14. [1934] 2 K.B. 394.

15. (1981), 34 B.C.L.R. 62, affirmed (1983), 24 C.C.L.T. 6.

16. (1988), 33 B.C.L.R. (2d) 160.

17. [1981] 5 W.W.R. 97, affirmed (1982), 136 D.L.R. (3d) 11.

18. *Dyck v. Manitoba Snowmobile Association Inc. and Wood* (1985), 18 D.L.R. (4th) 635.

19. (1992), 74 B.C.L.R. (2d) 159.

20. (1994), C934644 (B.C.S.C.).
21. (1991), C900215 (B.C.S.C.).
22. (1996), C922041 (B.C.S.C.).
23. (1997), Kelowna 26627 (B.C.S.C.).
24. [1918] A.C. 837.
25. Vancouver Reg. No. C927644, September 13, 1994.
26. *Dyck v. Manitoba Snowmobile Association* (1985).
27. Madam Justice Huddart in *Knowles v. Whistler Mountain Ski Corporation* (1990) as she described the concept of unconscionability.
28. [1989] 1 S.C.R. 426.
29. (1978), 9 B.C.L.R. 166 (C.A.).
30. (1987), 40 C.C.L.T. 1 (B.C.C.A.).
31. (1993), 74 B.C.L.R. (2d) 224.
32. [1992] 1 S.C.R. 351 (S.C.C.).
33. See *Peters v. Parkway Mercury Sales Ltd.* (1974), 9 N.B.R. (2d) 288 (N.B.Q.B.), affirmed (1975), 10 N.B.R. (2d) 703 (N.B.C.A.).
34. At the time of this writing, the Law Reform Commission of British Columbia has been disbanded and no longer exists.
35. These are paraphrased versions.
36. *Stevens v. Howitt* (1969), 1 O.R. 761 (H.C.). The ground cited for refusing to enforce the parent's indemnity agreement was that it discouraged a parent from pursuing a minor's legal rights, and this was inconsistent with public policy. An analogy could be drawn to the unenforceability of indemnity terms in a separation agreement which operate to the disadvantage of the children from the marriage: *Cutler v. Cutler*, [1991] B.C.D. Civ. 1604-06 (S.C.).
37. Robert Kennedy (attorney), during a February 13, 2000, presentation at the Adventure Tourism Conference 2000 at the University College of the Cariboo, Kamloops, B.C.
38. Although there are a number of different waiver formats in use, the format and content of this waiver have been taken from one drafted by Robert Kennedy, Attorney; Alexander, Holburn, Beaudin & Lang in Vancouver, B.C. Please see an attorney prior to drafting your own waiver document.

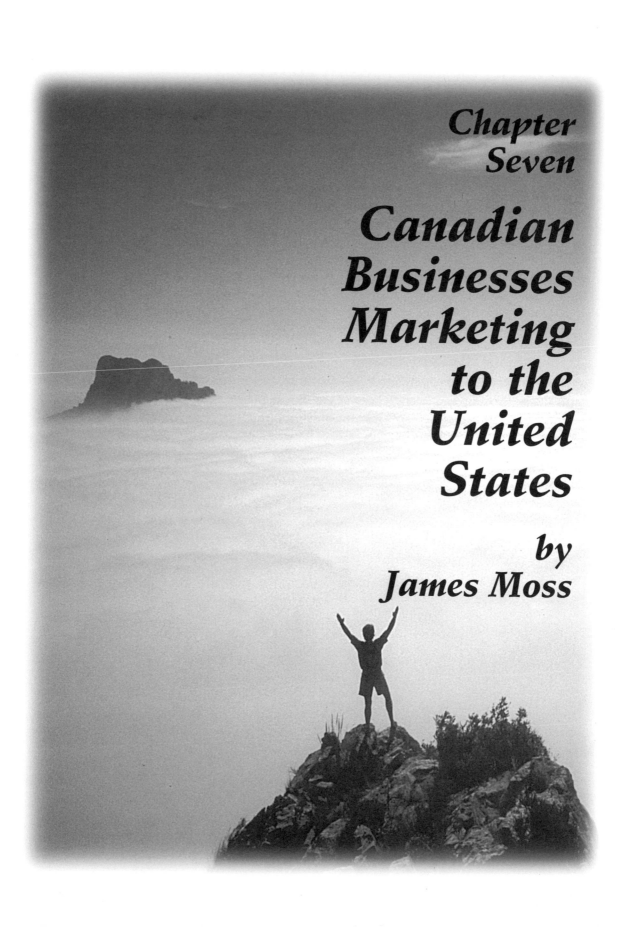

Chapter Seven

Canadian Businesses Marketing to the United States

by
James Moss

"Import Americans, import their lawsuits."

In the United States, the court system has become the act of first resort for any type of problem a person encounters. The courts tend to be viewed from two major economic perspectives: as a way of being reimbursed for expenses, or as a chance to receive a large amount of money. However, most lawsuits start because of bad service or a feeling of injustice.

Americans also feel that the United States system of justice should follow them wherever they travel, including the concept that any injury should be compensated and any injustice punished. What we have all seen in movies as the "ugly American" is played out every day around the world. Couple this with the idea that Canada is just like or is a part of the United States, and bringing Americans to Canada can be a litigation nightmare for all parties.

Often, Americans cannot understand why Canadians are not suing for millions and Canadians cannot understand why anyone would sue as easily as Americans do. A major factor in the litigation craze is the idea of United States justice. Justice and the foundation of the American government system are pounded into every child from the first grade onward. The basic belief that justice is an integral part of every American's existence eventually collides with the realities of life. The result in the U.S. today is a tidal wave of lawsuits to avenge every single perceived injustice. Combined with an overabundance of attorneys, this produces the recipe for an even worse disaster: that in American lawsuits the only winners might be the attorneys involved in those suits. (1)

One should never forget the penchant of Americans for litigation — or, more accurately, their penchant for justice. Any company doing business with Americans or marketing to Americans can be drawn into the U.S. litigation morass. However, with the appropriate information, it is a relatively simple process to market and serve Americans in Canada and around the world, to keep their lawsuits back in the U.S. and to not become a part of such suits.

The United States Court System

There are two basic, separate court systems in the U.S.: the state court system and the federal court system. Each deals with specific laws or parties; however, there is significant overlap in both the types of litigation and the litigants. Each system has a Trial Court and a Supreme Court; most have an Appellate Court. All litigation starts in the Trial Court. A party that is dissatisfied with a decision in the Trial Court can appeal that decision to the next court level. Normally this is the Appellate Court, but it may be the Supreme Court.

The state court system may also have various levels of trial courts. Most states have divisions between the courts based on the value of the lawsuit. Small-claims court is for small amounts normally between $2,500 and $5,000 in value. Additional courts may exist for amounts between specified values.

Both court systems deal with criminal actions, which will not be discussed here. However, any violation of the laws concerning access to federal lands and most state lands is a criminal act. Because the status of a Canadian business in the United States is that of a foreign national, the business may be required to post a bond before leaving the country, to be held until its return. Consider this when exploring options in leading commercial operations into the United States.

The State Court System

State courts deal with the violation of state laws and of the common law. The common law was originally the law of the Church and the king of England and was later adopted in the United States. The common law is now considered to be the law created by the courts. The majority of lawsuits in the United States are filed in the state court system.

> *If you are involved in a lawsuit with a U.S. citizen in the United States, you will have to hire a U.S. attorney. Make sure that your insurance policy will pay for this.*

The Federal Court System

Federal courts deal with the violation of federal laws and statutes. Examples of federal laws are civil-rights laws, tax laws and immigration statutes. Federal courts also deal with actions against or concerning the government — federal agencies such as the Bureau of Land Management, the National Park Service or the United States Forest Service. This is the court system that deals with illegal outfitting in a national park or national forest or on land under the jurisdiction of the Bureau of Land Management.

A lawsuit against a non-U.S.-based business can be removed to a federal court. The lawsuit will still be in the U.S.; however, the federal courts are considered less responsive to local pressures.

United States Courts and Canadians

Federal courts deal with large lawsuits between parties from two different states or between a United States party and a foreign-based business. A lawsuit between an American citizen and a Canadian business would likely be removed to the federal court system, although this may not always be the case. Any lawsuit started in the federal court system will be subject to federal laws.

Government Regulations Concerning Operation in the United States

In addition to the laws of the federal government, each one of the 50 states has its own laws concerning business in its jurisdiction. Before operating in the United States, a Canadian business may therefore need to register with or receive approval from up to 51 different governments.

The United States system of government is based on the idea that the state has the power unless that power has been given to the federal government. As such, each state has the right to control, license, regulate and tax the activities that occur within its boundaries. Activities crossing a state's boundaries may fall within the purview of both states involved in addition to the federal government.

> *The name of the government office responsible for recording and tracking corporations in the majority of American states is the Secretary of State.*

A business may have to register with the Secretary of State in each state in which it operates. (2) Registration requirements can range from simply filing a form listing the services the business intends to provide in the state — all the way to registering as a foreign corporation. Registering as a foreign corporation will require maintaining a place of business and hiring someone to be there. Space can be rented on a yearly basis from numerous business services in each state.

If you are transporting your clients, you may also need to deal with each state through which you are travelling. Federal and state public-utilities commissions regulate the transportation of people by commercial organizations.

Land Access

Private Land

As long as you have permission, there are no issues for Canadian businesses operating on private land in the United States. Permission can be as simple as a verbal okay, but you should formalize this in writing, preferably before leaving Canada. Most private land, however, does not have the features that people are seeking for outdoor recreation. Many areas that do have those features may not be accessible to everyone.

State Land

Land owned or controlled by a state government usually has similar restrictions and requirements to those applying on federal land. State recreational areas also tend to be highly patrolled because there is often more money available for recreational programs and enforcement than in federal jurisdictions.

Federal Land

All commercial (3) access to federal lands requires a permit. These permits may have different names — for example: Incidental Business Permit, Concessionaire's Contract or Special Use Permit. They require advance application and proof of financial ability and prior experience. Many take years of work to obtain. Most high-use areas impose limits on the number of permits issued. However, numerous permits are available for land areas in less-desired locations. The exception to this rule is whitewater rivers, which have been fully permitted for several years.

A foreign corporation may hold a permit. There is no restriction on ownership of a permit by a foreign business in the United States.

Technically, a permit is not *owned* by the permittee. The permit is a licence to access the area and by law has no value. However, the licence is transferable upon the sale of the business and on approval by the permitting agency. In numerous situations, a permitted business will sell at a price far in excess of the value of its assets because of the "actual" value of its permit.

Every land-management agency has its own permit process, which is controlled by regulations issued in Washington, D.C. However, each local district or park within that agency interprets the permit process in its own way; some local agencies construe the process strictly, while many do not. If the permit requires a specific application to be completed, the application is usually construed quite thoroughly.

> *A corporation not started or filed in a particular state is called a foreign corporation by that state, even if it is still a United States corporation. The term "foreign corporation" will therefore refer to a corporation that is incorporated in the United States and not in the state being discussed. The term "foreign business" will be used to refer to a business based outside of the United States.*

Working in the United States

Teaming up with an American Operation

The easiest way for a Canadian business to operate in the United States is to team up with an American operation that has the necessary permits. In this way, the business is able to place another defensive wall between itself and a possible lawsuit and it gains access to more areas in the United States.

A Canadian business can accomplish this in four ways:
❖ by booking clients through the American operation
❖ by taking its clients to the American operation and working as an employee of the American operation
❖ by establishing an American corporation and operating with its own permits in the United States
❖ by operating a Canadian business in the United States

Booking Clients through an American Operation

The easiest and safest way to carry out business in the United States is to simply "book" clients with a United States operation. The client writes a cheque to the Canadian business, which takes a commission and then forwards the balance to the American outfitter. This relationship can be beneficial if the American-based operation provides the same services as the Canadian-based operation.

Under federal law, the American operator, not the Canadian business, will be running the operation.

❖ The Canadian business incurs little cost and hassle.
❖ The Canadian business remains in Canada.
❖ The clients will be clients of the American business.
❖ The employees will be employees of the American business.
❖ The United States operator will have total control of the program.
❖ The Canadian business minimizes its risk and its exposure to a lawsuit from the United States.

Taking Clients and Working in the United States

This second option is chosen by many United States operators who want to work in Canada and vice versa. In this situation, the Canadian business takes its clients to the United States and operates under the American operator's permit.

❖ The Canadian business has high costs.
❖ Clients may write cheques to either the Canadian or the American business.
❖ The clients will be clients of the American business.
❖ The employees will be employees of the American business.
❖ The employees must be qualified to work in the United States.
❖ The employees must pay United States taxes on their earnings.
❖ The American and Canadian business insurance policies apply.
❖ The American operator will be in control of the operation.
❖ The American operator will be liable to the land manager.
❖ The Canadian business has legal exposure; however, the American business has greater exposure, and the Canadian business is behind it.

Owning an American Corporation

The third approach to carrying out business in the United States is to establish an American presence through an American corporation that is owned separately by the Canadian business.

❖ The Canadian business has high costs.
❖ The Canadian business is protected if the American corporation is set up properly. The American business has high legal exposure.
❖ United States taxes must be paid.
❖ The American business requires its own insurance policy.
❖ The American business must have its own United States permits.
❖ The American business may be set up with most of its assets being owned by the Canadian business.

Operating a Canadian Business in the United States

The final option for a Canadian business is to operate in the United States just as it operates in Canada. This option reduces overall costs, but the increased risks involved in a United States lawsuit may not justify the cost reduction.

❖ The business incurs lower overall costs.
❖ The business pays taxes in both countries.
❖ The business holds United States operating permits.
❖ The business will likely have both a Canadian and United States business policy.
❖ Employees must pay United States taxes on their United States earnings.
❖ The Canadian business is placing Canadian assets at risk in the case of a United States lawsuit.

The Duty of a United States Outfitter or Guide

United States law requires a high standard of care when dealing with customers, and an outfitter or guide has a considerable duty to his or her guests. The outfitter is responsible for the guests from the moment they are met and start on the adventure to the moment they leave to go home. This period during which the outfitter accepts responsibility is defined by the actions and decisions of the guest — not the outfitter.

Because the outfitter is familiar with the territory, the activity and the equipment whereas the guest is not, the outfitter bears the responsibility of keeping the guests safe. The outfitter must warn the guest of any known and unknown hazards involved in the trip.

Importing Americans to Canada

Importing Americans means importing lawsuits, unless you take steps to have United States lawsuits left at the border. Some businesses decide that the cost of preventing lawsuits or the lost income from such measures is not worth the effort. They would rather rely on their insurance policies and luck than take preventative steps to prevent litigation.

Compare the loss of business to the time you might spend in court defending a lawsuit: For someone with a significant injury and lost work, you will probably be in trial for ten days; that is ten days away from your business. For each day you are on the stand, you will normally spend three days preparing for your testimony. In a ten-day trial, you will be on the stand a minimum of one day. You will also be deposed for a day, which will also require three days of preparation. Add to this the time you spend with your attorney and time spent answering discovery and finding documents. This will add a minimum of another week. You have now lost a minimum of 24 days from your business. Add to this the time your staff spends in deposition and with your attorney, in addition to the lost time they incur because of your absence, and the total lost time can be considerable. Finally, add the negative feelings, fear and uncertainty that trial produces, and your entire business can fail because you have not created a program to stop litigation. From this perspective, there would have to be a considerable amount of business at stake in order to justify failing to prevent one lawsuit.

Turning someone away because he or she does not want to sign your document becomes easy compared to losing time and money in defending a suit from an injured client. Although it is impossible to calculate the number of people who decide not to attend a program, it is possible to gauge the effect those same people could have on your business. The cost of interrupting a trip to remove an unhappy, dissatisfied or scared client will always exceed the possible lost income. If you take the steps to market a great program, participants who enjoy your program will promote it. The alternative is a group of angry, disappointed people who feel they were misled. Free promotion is always better than disappointment.

Marketing to Americans

A business' marketing program can import a lawsuit without bringing American clients to Canada. If the business has the necessary minimum contacts with the United States, it can be brought into the United States with a lawsuit. Minimum contact is defined as:

> a. advertising in the United States
> b. advertising in American magazines
> c. advertising in magazines aimed at American citizens
> d. following up advertising with brochures
> e. calling American citizens
> f. entering the United States in order to market to customers
> g. not distinguishing the business as a non–United States–based operation

Legal Defenses

Assumption-of-risk Defense

In the United States, assumption of risk is an available defense used against a United States lawsuit. In Canada, assumption of risk is not as successful as a defense.

> **Assumption of risk is now legally called "contributory negligence" or "comparative negligence" in some American states. The legal application is different in each case, but the basic concept is the same.**

The basis for this defense is that the person who was injured knew what he or she was doing and voluntarily undertook the activity that led to the injury. It is a difficult defense to use because the injured party, the plaintiff, will always say that he or she did not understand the risks involved, even though the defendant adventure business may well have worked hard at informing its guests in this regard.

Assumption of risk is a question for the trier of fact. The trier of fact is the person who hears the case, the witnesses and the arguments. In most cases, this is a jury. However, in some cases, when the trial is to the court, the trier of fact is a judge. Because the trier of fact must hear all sides and all the evidence in order to determine whether the injured guest assumed the risk, the defendant in a lawsuit involving assumption of risk will very likely go to trial in most states. The judge or jury will decide whether the plaintiff fully understood the nature and effect of his or her actions.

There are two effective ways used both to educate the client and to later prove the client's exposure to that knowledge at trial: releases and videotaped instructions.

A release that indicates the risks of the activity goes a long way in showing, through a document signed by the client, that he or she knew and understood the risks of participating in a particular program. It is impossible to list every possible risk of an outdoor activity; however, information about the major risks and the common risks can adequately be covered in half a page.

The alternative is to show every client a videotape of the possible risks. For example, the Professional Paddlesports Association (PPA) (4) developed a video with the American Canoe Association and the United States Coast Guard which explains the risks of canoeing to clients. The video presents the most common risks of canoeing and paddling techniques and stresses that the canoeist is responsible for his or her own actions.

In the United States, assumption of risk is the only written defense that is available in a suit by a minor. A minor cannot contract, therefore a release is not a defense to a suit by a minor. Minors can, however, understand and assume the risks of their activities. A document written at a tenth-grade level or lower can be read and understood by most minors in the eighth grade, providing a defense to a lawsuit. A video shown to minors may be even more effective for younger clients.

> *In the years since the implementation of the PPA National Livery Safety System Video, there have been no lawsuits against an outfitter using the video. In each of two cases where an injured party contacted an attorney, once the attorney received a copy of the release signed by the client and a copy of the video viewed by the client, the possible claims disappeared.*

The concept of assumption of risk goes further than a legal defense. It is a way of preventing litigation before it starts, and of stopping potential litigants from leaving the United States in the first place. By totally explaining the risk, you are allowing your possible clients to honestly evaluate that risk. Clients who take a trip only to find out in the middle of it that they do not want to expose themselves to the level of risk and therefore want to leave pose a real hazard to all participants and to the trip itself. These people are more susceptible to accidents because fear tends to control their actions. They are unable to fully participate in the activities, causing frustration for the group and possibly a change in the itinerary. By informing your potential clients of the risks involved, you are weeding out these problems in advance and reducing the possibility of a lawsuit.

Finally, you have an ethical duty to explain the risks to potential clients. For example: Parents should know what their children are going to undertake. They can then decide if the risk is acceptable to them. If a child is injured and his or her parents were uninformed, they will blame you, not the child, for hiding the risk from them. A release or a written assumption-of-risk document requiring a parent's signature will allow a parent to make the required decision.

Ensuring assumption of risk, whether in writing, through the presentation of a video or over the telephone, will assist you in deterring unsuitable people and possible litigants from taking your trips.

Legal Release

A critical component in the defense strategy is a release. Releases are also known as waivers, or covenants not to sue, among several other names. Regardless of the term used, the document's purpose is to inform the client of the possible risk and to transfer liability to the person incurring the injury.

A release is a contract between two parties. One party is the adventure business, while the other is the guest. Each party agrees in writing to bear the cost itself of any accident, injury or loss it may incur. Because a release is a contract, contractual legal requirements must be met. Money must flow between the parties, creating a business-client relationship, and one party or both must receive a benefit from the transaction. The release must bear the signature of the person against whom it is being used, i.e. the client.

Most releases stop at this point. However, effective releases include additional language in order to ensure that the parties understand all the damages they may sustain and the penalties for violating the contract. In the United States, most people look at a release as a way of preventing lawsuits.

Releases are used as defenses to win trials in the United States. A release can also be used in a motion for summary judgement in order to stop the lawsuit before trial. Another possible use of a release is in positioning the defendant to negotiate a settlement for minimal or nuisance damages.

Releases often prevent situations from resulting in litigation. When people remember that they signed a legal document stating they could not sue, they frequently decide not to pursue the case. Although there is no way of quantifying how often this occurs, it is unquestionably one of the benefits provided by releases to an adventure business.

The release also provides a benefit to the client by clearly explaining the risks of the activity. It allows the client to evaluate the actual risk and to make a decision as to whether or not he or she wishes to assume that risk. It is always better for the client to decide not to participate in the trip in the first place than to decide halfway through the activity that he or she does not want to be exposed to the risk. The worst type of lawsuit is that from an injured party who had no desire to continue the activity once he or she found out what was involved. Without the necessary information to make an informed consent, the client feels misled by the outfitter, which increases the chances of suit and intensifies the animosity that leads to a bitter lawsuit.

The law is never a firm line on the beach. It is a group of known dos and don'ts, with each new set of facts requiring understanding and interpretation as to how the law is going to be applied and how it will arrive at its outcome. The law concerning releases is the same. There is no Rosetta stone explaining exactly how a release should be written. However, reading and reviewing the decisions of various courts on why they have accepted or rejected a particular release provides insight about ways to write a release and about what the document should include or exclude. It is for this reason that your release should be examined and updated each year by your attorney. A local case may alert an attorney to what the judge wants to see in the release. A major decision by a higher court may totally change the way in which the language is interpreted or the way in which the release is going to be applied. Because of this, your attorney should examine your release regularly in order to maintain its effectiveness.

In this regard, you may need to have your release reviewed by a United States attorney, or to have two separate releases: one prepared by a Canadian attorney for Canadians and one prepared by a United States attorney for use by Americans. This may lead to some confusion; colour-coding your documents will make it easier to grab, for instance, light red documents for Canadians and light blue documents for Americans. On the surface, Canadian and United States laws may appear similar; however, the differences may mean the difference between winning and losing a case.

Jurisdiction Clause

The jurisdiction clause is the most important part of any contract when dealing with Americans and one should be included in all marketing agreements and releases. A jurisdiction clause states that the parties agree in advance that any lawsuit will be held in the stated jurisdiction. For example: The jurisdiction clause might state that all lawsuits concerning any part of the agreement will be held in Kamloops, British Columbia, Canada. A Texas tourist who is hurt will then have to find an attorney in Kamloops who is willing to sue a Kamloops business.

In addition to forcing the plaintiff to come to your "backyard" to sue you, you will be dealing with a judge or jury of local citizens. Juries composed of locals will be less likely to award damages against a local company. The plaintiff will be faced with additional costs and an uphill battle against the locals, and so may be discouraged from attempts to litigate. For example: The National Outdoor Leadership School (NOLS) was named in 1998 as a defendant in a lawsuit filed by an injured student in New York City. The injured student lived in New York and had contracted to take the NOLS trip from New York. However, the NOLS agreement stated that any lawsuit must be held in Lander, Wyoming. NOLS presented a motion requiring that the contract terms be enforced and the lawsuit be dismissed in New York and started in Lander, Wyoming. The lawsuit was dismissed, and nothing else was ever done. The injured student in New York did not want to find a Lander attorney.

Choice-of-law Clause

This may be the second most important clause in a contract with Americans. Canadian businesses are used to dealing with and understanding Canadian law. A choice-of-law clause states that the laws of Canada will be the laws applied in the lawsuit. American attorneys are reluctant to learn new laws and will find it difficult to sue using Canadian law.

Canadian law also limits the damages that are recoverable by an injured plaintiff; awards for pain and suffering and emotional distress are significantly reduced compared to those in the

> *Punitive damages are damages awarded to punish the defendant because his or her actions were so egregious. These damages are not covered by insurance policies and are not dischargeable in the case of bankruptcy.*

United States. When punitive damages are applied in Canada according to Canadian laws, an American attorney, faced with learning another forum's laws and not receiving a large judgement, will not be interested in taking on a lawsuit.

Liquidated-damages Clause

Liquidated damages are damages that are agreed to in advance by contract. They may be a specific amount or they may be based on an easily ascertainable value.

In some cases, a liquidated-damages clause is a double-edged sword; however, if written effectively, it can be used to scare lawsuits away. The clause states that, if the defendant is forced to defend a lawsuit and is successful in that defense, the defendant will be awarded the costs of defending the lawsuit, including attorney fees. In many cases, attorney fees can be in excess of $100,000 US.

Arbitration Clause

An arbitration clause requires that, instead of going to court, the dispute is placed in front of a neutral party who makes the decision. The arbitration clause is effective because it reduces the costs incurred compared to the time and expense involved in carrying through with a lawsuit. The clause is also beneficial to the operator if the rules governing the arbitration require a commercial arbitrator. Commercial arbitrators are usually more conservative than a jury.

Arbitration clauses are only effective if they are binding on both parties, which means that there needs to be a statute or law stating that the clause must be acted on and cannot be changed by the courts.

The North American Free Trade Agreement

The North American Free Trade Agreement (NAFTA) is a treaty between Canada, the United States and Mexico. NAFTA has provisions for doing business between countries on all levels including tourism. Any commercial agreement between businesses may fall under the purview of NAFTA. NAFTA requires mandatory arbitration, limited damages and other ways to resolve disputes without litigation. It is also stipulated that the meetings of any arbitration be closed-door and that no appeal be available on decisions. United States law is not followed; each argument under NAFTA is argued on its own basis through the application of international law, which entails fewer torts and is less oriented towards the injured person. In addition, any dispute resolved in such a way that the law of the land is applied in an unfair way may be brought against the winning party's country for damages. If you are entering into a long-term contract with a U.S.-based company, you should examine NAFTA for help in correctly completing the agreement.

Conclusion

Dealing with Americans is often necessary due to the size of the market they represent. You should not be discouraged by the threat of litigation. Nor should you enter into this market without understanding and preparing for the risks involved. Just as with the risks inherent in the activities we promote, prior knowledge of those risks and of the ways to deal with Americans can make the business opportunities well worth the effort.

Notes to Chapter Seven

1. Some theorize that television contributed to this mess; they argue that the increase in litigation is due to lawyers advertising on television in the U.S. However, it is likely that the advertising simply made it easier to find a lawyer. Television certainly did contribute to the increase in the number of lawyers in the U.S.: during the 1980s, the desire in young people to become an attorney jumped from 10th to first place in career choices for more than five consecutive years with the airing of "L.A. Law" and other legal shows.
2. This text will not inquire into any issues concerning customs and immigration.
3. Although each of the land-management agencies defines "commercial" differently, the term generally refers to any activity that is not shared-cost (i.e. common adventure). Indications of a commercial operation include: one or more persons in the group is being paid; there is a difference among the amounts being paid by various group members, or someone is going for free; someone is making a profit; and the vehicle being used is registered as commercial or has lettering on its side.
4. The Professional Paddlesport Association was formerly known as the National Association of Canoe Liveries and Outfitters (NACLO).

Chapter Eight

Risk Management

What Risk Management Is

Risk management is a rational approach taken by a business in order to deal with risk. It is about managing or optimizing risks; it is not necessarily about eliminating them, because risk is inherent in adventure activities — and should remain so. Risk management is concerned with all types of risk, regardless of whether or not they are insurable, and involves choosing appropriate techniques for dealing with the hazards faced by a business.

Risk management should be looked on as a process, not as any individual technique, item or document. The risk-management process consists of determining the exposure levels that are acceptable to the planning organization and its guests, identifying hazards to the business, evaluating those hazards, selecting finance and control alternatives, implementing mitigation strategies and planning appropriate responses to emergency incidents. Ultimately, the long list of steps to be followed in risk management will be determined by the first: deciding on exposure levels that are acceptable to the individual organization and its guests.

It is important to grasp the concept that the level of risk management applied is relative to the tolerance of a specific business and its guests for risk, which can vary substantially from one operator to another. If risk is mitigated to a point below a particular tolerance, guest experiences will be affected. There is no expectation by the court that all risk will be eliminated from adventure activities:

> It is not contended that the defendants had a duty to ensure that their guests were kept away from all places where avalanches could occur. In the context of helicopter skiing that would be impossible. I think it correct to say the duty of care which lay on the defendants was not to expose their guests to risks regarded in the business as unreasonably high, whether from avalanche or any other hazard to which participants in the sport are normally exposed. To enjoy the excitement of skiing in mountain wilderness areas participants are necessarily exposed both to risks which the careful skier is able to avoid and certain risks also which such skiers may be unable to avoid, including some risk of being caught in an inescapable avalanche. (1)

Why Risk Management?

Business managers, trip planners and guides all have responsibility for dealing with risks during the planning and operation of their businesses and trips. They are responsible for carrying out due diligence in risk management in order to not unduly expose themselves, their organizations, their guides or their customers to hazard. They are also required to mitigate these risks as much as possible, and to adequately respond to incidents that may occur as a result of the business' operations.

Bill March on Risk

Adventure and risk have been from the very beginning of man's existence an integral part of his character and personality. The acts of protection, defending territorial rights and foraging for food were some of the daily risks taken by early man. Dr. Sol Rosenthal coined the term "risk exercise," describing man's need for a well calculated risk taking on a physical and mental basis. When we stop doing things that require us to stretch our physical and mental resources, to push ourselves beyond the point where we are completely safe, we are being unnatural in terms of our natural heritage. Today, however, the growth of government at the expense of individual freedom is a force that threatens to pervade all aspects of our lives including our recreation. The concept of the "common good" as decreed by experts is beginning to take precedence over the development of individual decision making. George Leonard in *The Ultimate Athlete*, says, "When society through its agencies protects people from dangers created by nature or by other people, it is taking care of its proper business. But when it begins protecting people from themselves, from their own urges for experience and adventure, it is partaking in a particularly dangerous course." The problem is, of course, where to draw the line between the distinctions defined by Leonard.

A study of recorded human history reveals adventure to be a recurring theme through man's culture ... adventure has become fashionable and has found a wide application in many different enterprises. The booming of adventure travel firms, the development of special wilderness seminars for business executives, the application of the wilderness experience to the rehabilitation of juvenile delinquents, the tremendous increase in agency participation in outdoor pursuits extending through the education spectrum from school to university. What can we, as educators, do in deciding what is an acceptable level of risk?

The *Oxford Dictionary* defines adventure as follows: a chance of danger or loss; risk; jeopardy; a hazardous enterprise or performance. The essence of the wilderness experience is a voluntary calculated exposure to a potentially harmful situation with a degree of risk. It is essential for climbers to cultivate a sound philosophy and adopt a healthy attitude in the approach to risk in their sports.

Many guidelines and program plans have been developed for the safe teaching of adventure activities and have generally resulted in highly structured teaching environments which are self defeating in generating self responsibility and independent thinking. True safety ultimately does not depend on bureaucratic dos and don'ts and magical preconceived educational recipes but on the development of the ability and judgement of the individual. People must be exposed to progressively more demanding situations commensurate with their abilities. In short, they must come to understand themselves and establish a balance between their "inner self" and their outer actions or adventures. This can only be effectively achieved through ... situations where we learn independently from our own "mini epics." The educational process should concentrate on providing sufficient information to keep epics "non fatal." (2)

Perspectives on Risk Management

Risk management is practised for a variety of reasons, and a business operator can easily fall into the trap of adopting a narrow view of its purpose. Often the first reason that comes to mind is protecting a business from litigation: did the business conform to statute and common law, and if it is sued will it win? This view is commonly expanded to include financial considerations: will the business survive the incident, and how can it reduce the financial consequences?

A higher-level consideration is the public-relations impact: how will the business look in the public eye, and will the incident affect its image? A discerning operator will recognize that accidents result in greater publicity and media coverage and very often increase call volume for a business. The way an incident is handled becomes important in determining how the public perceives the business. Good accident management often results in increased business and public attention. Business operators who have experienced a commercial adventure accident frequently say, "It doesn't matter what they say about you, as long as they spell your business name and the town you are from correctly." Accidents tend to result in widespread media attention and in publicity that most businesses could not afford to buy. Adventure consumers have short memories and a strong affinity for self-denial: "An accident won't happen to me."

The highest level of scrutiny for evaluating a risk-management program is likely the ethical and moral one: Did the business display morally excellent behaviour within the profession? This judgement by peers is made according to such criteria as justice, virtue, integrity, honesty and fairness. How does the industry as a whole view the risk management carried out by the business, and were these criteria met? For example: The inclusion of negligence in assumption-of-risk statements in waivers is allowed by some legal jurisdictions, (3) but is it really ethical or moral — and a principle on which the adventure industry should be able to rely? One perspective, held by an increasing number of legal jurisdictions, (4) and operators, is that requiring clients to sign away their rights to sue, even where the business is negligent, is unethical — if not immoral. Risk-management considerations at this level look at whether or not the business complies to the expanded, ideal code of moral principles associated with a profession and whether or not the techniques applied conform with generally accepted societal standards of goodness or rightness.

Ultimately, risk management should create a balance between legal strategies intended to protect the worth and life of the business, and the underlying professional and ethical values of its personnel. Whether the marketplace and the insurance industry will accept the increased cost and higher risk of such an ethical approach remains to be seen.

Risk-management Techniques

Risk management combines both risk-control and risk-financing techniques. Risk-control techniques are intended to reduce or eliminate incidents; they include exposure avoidance, loss prevention, loss reduction and loss sharing. Risk-financing techniques deal with financial

Worth Considering: The Moral Underpinning of Risk Management

A business operator's decision about whether or not to use a given risk-management tool sometimes boils down to a simple matter of logistics and economics. The documentation recommended adds to the workload and may seem like pointless bureaucracy. However, it is worth considering a few very important underlying issues. Should these drawbacks be the criteria behind the decision to implement risk management, or is there a higher purpose for striving for excellence in every aspect of a program — such as reducing suffering and loss of human life?

Risk management is too often portrayed primarily as a lawsuit mitigator. Lawsuit mitigation alone is not a good enough reason for implementing a given risk-management tool. The tool must serve a higher purpose. Take, for example, one of the most difficult aspects of risk management: liability-release forms. Release forms can be a logistical nuisance and can create public-relations nightmares, but let us consider one core benefit of using them: The more participants know about the activity in which they are about to engage, the less likely they are to do something that would contribute to their own demise. It is no surprise that the incidence of serious accidents is much lower for instructional programs than for other programs, because instructional programs usually spend more time giving their participants a thorough coverage of the basic skills. A well-written liability-release form helps to inform participants about the nature of the activity and about ways in which they can function more safely in the relevant environment. The fact that the forms are also great defense tools in dealing with frivolous lawsuits is simply an additional benefit.

Participants have to take a degree of responsibility for their decisions. When someone voluntarily participates in an activity with known inherent risks and gets hurt through no one's intentional wrongdoing, the business should not be held responsible. Release forms enable companies to stress this to their participants.

Every trip should also have an appropriate emergency and evacuation plan for all activities and the areas in which they take place. One approach you can take is to hypothetically put your family members in the picture as participants. What level of professionalism and emergency preparedness would you expect of the guides/instructors in that situation?

As outdoor professionals, we have focused a lot of attention on the development of our skills. The more obvious technical skills such as climbing, paddling and biking are of great importance. As well, strong interpersonal skills such as counselling, facilitation and conflict resolution are essential to anyone professionally involved in this industry. Risk management is yet another area of competence that needs to be added to a person's tick list of outdoor skills. Risk-management thinking is actually nothing new. The best programs have been doing it for years without knowing what it was called. Good risk management ties together all the highly diverse components of outdoor education/recreation and complements the whole.

While any effective risk-management procedure has many purposes, the reduction of injuries being perhaps the most obvious, the issue of personal integrity and craftsmanship is also important. Good risk management is satisfying and rewarding — and integrity is reason enough for doing anything.

Will Leverette

Marty von Neudegg on Risk

The expected and usual thing to say in the wilderness industry is that we're in the business of minimizing risks. Let me state clearly and unequivocally that we are not in the business of minimizing risks. To many people that statement is tantamount to heresy: how can you run a business and how can you have any guests if you cannot give them some assurance that you're minimizing the risks in your sport? We don't minimize the risks, and we're busy. That's not to imply that we're unsafe.

The definition of "to minimize" is "to reduce to a minimum, to estimate at the smallest amount possible." Well, in our business, to get to a state of the smallest amount of risk possible would by necessity mean not to venture out at all into the wilderness. To minimize the risk would be to avoid it completely; to reach the promised land of minimal risk, we would all be forced into following the maxim of Al Capone, the famous operator of many one-way tours, who said, "Nobody moves, nobody gets hurt."

So if we do not minimize the risk, just what is it that we do? At CMH (Canadian Mountain Holidays) we believe we optimize the risk. And the definition of "optimize" is "to make the most effective use of the particular situation." And this definition truly approaches reality. When children learn to climb up high places or ride a bicycle, they cannot do it without fear or accidents. They are learning what scares them and what can hurt them. But more importantly they are learning how to find an acceptable level of risk, appropriate to them as an individual. Humans are not a culture of people who want no risk... To the contrary, we are and always have been a species that's been willing to accept risk at many different levels. We all find a target of risk that's acceptable to us. Interestingly, that target can shift very easily, so, for instance, the little old lady who drives down the highway at 50 miles an hour may feel perfectly safe and be inside her target. But if she now gets a seat belt and air bag and ABS brakes and very little traffic, she steps on it and now she's driving 70 miles an hour. She's found a new target of risk. What's changed? The activity of driving is still the same. Is she truly any safer? Well, probably not. The gadgets that made her drive faster just moved the edge but the end result of a crash at higher speed is the same. What did she gain in real safety? Nothing. She just feels safer, and thinks she has minimized her risk. What she's really doing is making the best out of the situation and maybe, just maybe, getting a little bit more out of life.

So this all leads to what we're faced with in the heli-ski business. New technology, new forms of snow science make us feel safer. Added to the mix are the heightened expectations of our guests for more skiing. But let's not forget that we're running a business. Because we want our guests to be happy and return to us each year, we're forced to find the target of risk just on the other side of fun, but still on this side of disaster.

We face many dangers with our guests. They derive considerable enjoyment from these dangers when they're all linked together and they still produce a nice safe run. These dangers, no matter how real, are often completely transparent to the guests. For heli-skiers it's a state of awareness coupled with a healthy dose of willful blindness. They know the danger's there someplace. They can't see it for themselves. They like it that way. But they accept the risk as part of the experience.

In a paper presented at the 1996 Annual Snow Science Workshop, Walter Bruns, our chief operating officer at CMH, said, "Insofar as risks can be perceived, control can be exercised over them. The degree of control corresponds with the extent of perception. Control takes the form of avoidance, mitigation, or conscious acceptance in the choices that are made. Where risks are not perceived, the de facto choice is tacit acceptance. One cannot avoid or mitigate that which is not perceived. Tacit acceptance of unperceived risk simply acknowledges its existence and implicitly accepts potential consequences without further knowledge. This so-called residual risk is pervasive in the background of any mountain guiding situation."

It's foreign to many people's thinking, who are not mountain people, that we can have a group of guests who choose to accept this residual risk and also choose enjoyment over complete safety. But the truth is that safety and enjoyment often work against each other. The more safe a run becomes, the less fun it is. If it's completely flat, it'd be completely safe, but who's going to pay $5,000 for a week of that? So I must emphasize that this does not make us or our skiers unsafe. In fact, I must emphasize very strongly that the collective efforts of our guides and our guests make us much safer. Within the bounds of what we know and what we can control, safety is always our first priority. We work diligently to get better at our craft and we work just as hard at educating our skiing clients about the risks they are about to assume.

As a corporation we must inform our guests that there are risks they must share with us. We inform them of the dangers in our brochures and we try to be very honest. We go so far as to print the actual number of fatalities we've suffered in 32 years of business. We ask them to sign a waiver which is designed to inform the guests of the dangers they will encounter. And yes, it can and does protect CMH in the event of an accident but the protection is founded on the basis of the guests knowing fully what they are getting themselves into. Without full information we have no protection. And when they arrive they are instructed on how to behave while skiing, what hazards to watch for, and how they will help us in a search in the event of an accident.

The question we are asked today is, "Whose risk is it?" Clearly, when a guest comes skiing with CMH, the answer is "all of ours." This means that the risk belongs to each individual and each corporation on that run that day. To pretend that the guide is fully accountable or that the guest must be held fully responsible is wrongheaded. The safety on the day is shared by all of us. We would not be there is it were not for the guests. They could not be there if it was not for us. And while the guides make all the decisions on where each run will be skied based upon factors which are optimized, the guests have the ultimate control in our business by not buying into one of our trips.

So, if, God forbid, we have an accident, please consider that as a guest you've chosen to share the risk with us. Do not sue us for the risk you have accepted as part of your life. Do not sue us knowing that your risk target brought you heli-skiing. Do not sue us for making the most effective use of our situation. And most of all, do not sue us for failing to minimize the risk. (5)

considerations and include risk transfer through insurance, risk transfer through contract, risk transfer through participant assumption, and risk retention on the part of the organization.

Figure 8-1 ❖ Risk Control and Risk Financing

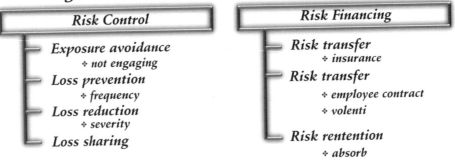

These risk-control and risk-financing techniques are carried out both before and after an incident through preventative strategies and response strategies. In addition, guides and business operators participate in pre- and post-incident activities throughout the entire risk-management process.

Figure 8-2 ❖ Incident-management Strategies

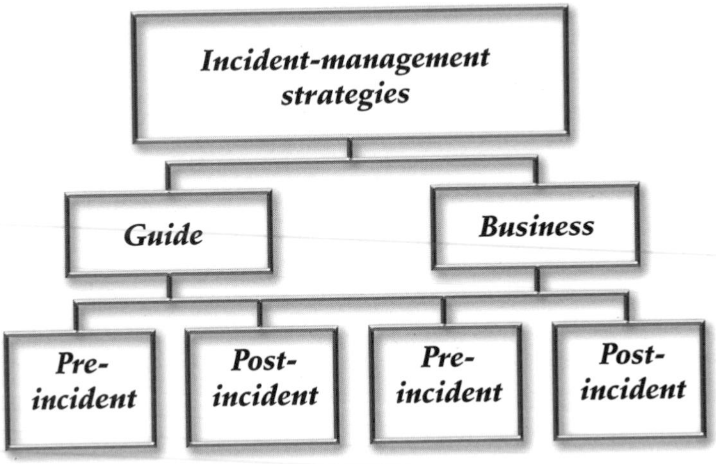

Risk-management Planning

Risk-management planning is carried out through the process of developing a series of planning and policy documents for a business. These documents may include any combination of materials developed in four main categories: general business concerns, trip planning, staff training and client materials.

Figure 8-3 ❖ Risk-management Documentation

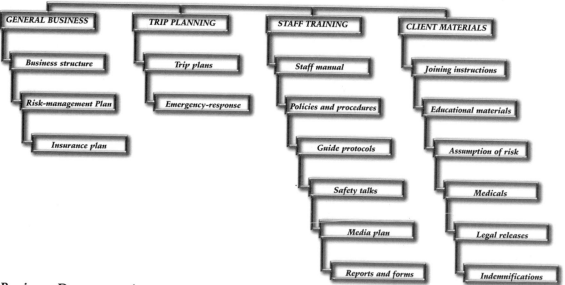

Business Documentation

General business documentation that also serves as risk-management documentation includes incorporation documents, a risk-management plan and an insurance plan. Incorporation documents play a part in business risk management because they deal with such relevant concerns as legal status, asset holdings, buy-out clauses and ownership structures — all areas that provide risk exposure to the ongoing business operations of the firm. The risk-management plan is a planning document that identifies hazards to the business and develops policies and strategies to deal with them. These hazards may include loss of permits, loss of insurance, vehicle accidents and undertrained staff. An insurance plan determines which assets and hazards to the business will be insured and what level of risk will be retained through insurance deductibles.

Trip-planning Documentation

Trip-planning documentation includes pre-trip plans and emergency-response plans. The purpose of these documents is to demonstrate that adequate planning has taken place before a trip's operation, to determine the logistics required to support a trip and to outline how the business will respond to emergencies caused by hazards during the trip.

Staff-training Documentation

The intent of developing staff-training materials such as staff manuals, policies and procedures, guide emergency protocols, safety-talk outlines, media plans and report formats is to provide adequate training and resources to front-line staff who are responsible for both preventing and responding to potential incidents.

Risk Management Simplified in Six Easy Steps

The success of any risk-management plan revolves largely around the understanding, simplification and implementation of a program that actually gets used by everyone in the organization. Many levels of complexity and detail can of course be applied, but the essential elements are actually fairly simple. Based on the examination of dozens of lawsuits against outfitters and on hundreds of risk-management consultations, the following is a list of important risk-management strategies that could be beneficial to most outfitters in the event that they are faced with litigation:

1. Develop a means to prove that guests were adequately warned and informed.

No more "My client was not adequately warned and informed, and therefore did not know what he or she was getting into." This is the single most common allegation against outfitters, and the most difficult one to disprove without some kind of documentation. There are many ways to go about ensuring the provision of adequate information. A business can design a basic safety-talk outline and laminate it on a small card as a reference for its guides in order to make sure that they do not forget important points; handouts containing pertinent safety information can be given out to participants prior to the trip; signs can be posted; a safety video can be produced. Any of a number of creative solutions can be used. Redundancy is always a good idea, too; it reduces the possibility of ambiguity.

2. Any guarantee of safety made in a business' literature or marketing materials is an open invitation to be sued.

The materials can mention such things as the business' excellent safety record, its extensive staff training and/or experience and its membership in professional trade organizations, without guaranteeing safety. Everything a business does to make sure its guests know what they are getting into and what is required of them will work in its favour. This includes all printed materials and advertising — even scripts for staff to use in order to answer frequently asked questions.

3. All field staff must have current training in basic first aid.

This is the industry standard, required by all government permitting agencies; it must be adhered to. In fact, in today's world, given the numerous recreation-industry-specific first-aid courses now widely available, it could be argued that basic first-aid training does not meet the prevailing industry standard. Think of it this way: would you want one of your own family members to be attended to by someone with basic first aid or by someone with a higher level of training?

4. The business should develop a written emergency/evacuation plan for all areas and activities to be used.

The plan does not have to be rigid or precisely followed in all situations, as this would be unrealistic and impossible. It does need to contain general guidelines and information that field staff will find useful in an emergency situation.

5. One good witness statement will shut down a frivolous lawsuit faster, more cheaply and less painfully than will anything else.

The business must have some means of tracking the names, addresses and phone numbers of all the participants in its activities. Staff should be alerted to the critical importance of witnesses and trained to look for opportunities to obtain names and phone numbers of independent persons such as private recreationists who might have seen the accident.

6. The business must use a properly drafted liability-release form.

The old adage "They aren't worth the paper they are printed on," may have been true in the '70s, but it does not apply today. The courts are increasingly supportive of the doctrine of the express (written) release. The mere threat that a particular release may work as a defense in a given situation is sometimes enough to persuade the litigation attorney in a frivolous cause of action (personal-injury lawsuit) to advise his or her client to be satisfied with the excess medical benefit offered by the business' liability-insurance policy. Does the client really want to spend the time and money to find out whether or not the release will be upheld? Often the answer is no.

These types of risk-management strategies are easy to develop and implement and are important to use for many reasons. The fear of litigation alone is not a good enough reason to do anything. If a tool doesn't serve the larger purpose of providing safer, better-organized, less problematic programming, then it is not worth adopting. The bottom line must always be to do everything possible to reduce the likelihood of human pain and suffering. All outfitters should aim to have better-warned and -informed participants. Safety talks, activity orientations, carefully drafted literature, and liability-release forms all contribute towards this goal. Emergency plans, and staff trained in first aid enable the outfitter to take care of people when the unfortunate does occur. The secondary benefit — that of strengthening the outfitter's position when faced with a frivolous lawsuit — is just a welcome bonus for doing the right thing!

Will Leverette

Using Incorporation to Limit Personal Exposure

There are a number of reasons for incorporating a business. The two most common are to either take advantage of corporate taxation rules in order to minimize income tax (becoming scarcer each year) or to use a corporation as a means of limiting personal exposure to legal liability arising from business debts or the execution of judgements. If a plaintiff is successful in obtaining a judgement against you and you have no insurance coverage or inadequate levels of insurance, then the plaintiff may execute his or her judgement against you in a variety of ways. These means can range from seizing your bank account to seizing and selling your personal assets such as your car, home, television, etc.

Incorporating your business is one way to protect your personal assets from being used to satisfy a judgement. As an owner of an incorporated business, it is highly unlikely (subject to certain exceptions outlined below) that you personally, rather than your business, will be held responsible for a negligent act. A corporation is considered to be a separate legal entity under the law. It is treated as a living and breathing person; it can own property, pay income taxes, be sued and even be charged with criminal offences and put to trial.

In incorporating a business, you take advantage of the "corporate veil". The corporate veil is a doctrine according to which, subject to certain exceptions, the courts will not look behind the company to reach those persons who stand behind it, such as owners or directors. The courts will restrict their scrutiny of the company's transgressions or debts to the company itself. In terms of executing a judgement against the company, this means that only the assets held by the company itself can be used to satisfy that judgement. The personal assets of the owners or directors cannot be attacked if the assets of the company prove insufficient to satisfy that obligation. The same cannot be said if you own an unincorporated business.

The assets of the business itself can be further protected through creating layers of corporations where one company (the holding company) owns the assets and leases them to a second company (the operating company), which actually conducts the business. Thus the assets of the holding company are not available for execution of a judgement or debt owed by the operating company.

As always, there are some exceptions that allow creditors to hold directors or owners of a corporation personally liable. This is called "piercing the corporate veil". Some exceptions are based upon reprehensible conduct of the owner/director, such as fraud. Other exceptions are for debts owed to government agencies, such as unpaid source deductions owed to Revenue Canada, unpaid GST, unpaid Provincial Sales Tax, etc. Other exceptions are legislated as being in the public interest such as directors being liable for up to six months of unpaid employee wages. The most common exception is where the owner/director contracts out of the protection provided by the corporate veil. This latter exception usually takes the form of personal guarantees issued by the owner/director (and even their spouses) to banks, suppliers etc. The savvy creditor will usually insist on personal guarantees before extending long-term credit to a corporation.

Despite the exceptions outlined above, the incorporation of a business is often a useful tool in limiting personal exposure to debts or judgements. This is especially true in businesses engaged in recreational activities that involve moderate or high levels of risk. It would be prudent to consult both a lawyer and an accountant if you are considering incorporating a business.

Don Blakely

Client Documentation

Materials that are developed for clients also act as risk-management documents because their intent is to educate the participant about what is involved in the trip. In addition, the effectiveness of any defense will rest largely on the preparedness of the guest, how well he or she understood the risks involved and how clearly these risks were accepted. Client documentation includes marketing materials, joining instructions, information packages and release contracts.

A well-organized and well-run business will develop and implement the complete spectrum of these planning materials, in all four areas.

Notes to Chapter Eight

1. *Scurfield v. Cariboo Helicopter Skiing Ltd.* (1993), 74 B.C.L.R. (2d) 224.
2. This section is taken in its entirety from a course handout used by Bill March at the University of Calgary in November 1977. It was later printed as "Adventure and Risk" by Bill March in the Alpine Club of Canada *Gazette*, 1, 1 (Summer 1986).
3. This refers to statements in legal releases such as "I understand and accept risks inherent in the activities ... including negligence on the part of the operator."
4. These jurisdictions include U.S. federal lands and, increasingly, Canadian federal lands. In addition, bodies such as the British Columbia Law Review Commission which have studied the law in this area suggest that the courts should not allow negligence to be included in assumption-of-risk statements, and that they should declare these statements "null and void" if they are included. This argument is based on ethical and moral considerations.
5. Marty von Neudegg is the vice-president and general counsel for Canadian Mountain Holidays (CMH). This article was originally presented at a panel discussion at the 1996 Banff Mountain Film Festival and was subsequently published in the August/September 1997 issue of *Explore* magazine.

Chapter Nine

Preparing Risk-management Documents

The chart entitled "Risk-management Documentation" on Page 103 shows the types of documents a business needs to develop in order to provide the level of information required by staff and guests and to cover any other risk-management-planning requirements. This chapter outlines the content of some of these documents.

The Risk-management Plan

The risk-management plan outlines the policies and procedures that a business will use in order to mitigate or respond to crisis and emergency situations affecting the company. It is a basic document that explains corporate philosophy and standard operating procedures to the reader. In addition, it identifies hazards to the business and outlines strategies for dealing with them. The process of writing a risk-management plan forces the business manager to think through individual and corporate philosophies, acceptable procedures and legal-liability ramifications, as well as specific emergency-response guidelines.

When writing a risk-management plan, it is important to keep in mind the multitude of potential uses for the document. Over its life, the plan may be used to supply policy information for business investors and owners, to provide procedural guidelines to employees, to form the basis for future emergency-response plans and — in the extreme case — to furnish legal protection. The document must be broad enough to cover these potential uses, but its wording must be chosen carefully. *Do not make statements in the plan that cannot, or will not, be adhered to!*

The following sections describe the standard risk-management plan. Include in the plan information that is useful to you while keeping in mind the legal requirements of your specific activities. In addition, write the risk-management plan with the understanding that it should concern itself with higher-level business hazards and how the business will respond to them. Trip-level hazards will be dealt with in a trip plan and in the trip plan's accompanying emergency-response plan.

Determining Risk-management Objectives

The first step in the risk-management process is to determine precisely what the planning organization expects its risk-management program to achieve. There is a tendency to look at this process as a series of isolated incidents rather than as a single problem. There is also a tendency to look at risk-management planning as a way of reducing all risks to the company. In adventure businesses, this is rarely the case. Risk-management objectives serve as a source of guidance for the people made responsible for those objectives and may later serve as a means of evaluating performance.

A *primary objective* of risk management is the goal of protecting employees, volunteers or guests from property loss, injury or death.

A *secondary objective* of risk management is to preserve the operations of an organization, whether it is a not-for-profit society, a business, an institution or a municipality. This implies avoidance of financial catastrophe that could result in significant loss, lawsuits or bankruptcy.

Other objectives of risk management are to carry out due diligence regarding professional planning procedures, to consider ethical and social responsibilities and to preserve good public relations.

Business Description

A risk-management plan is written for a specific business. It is necessary to identify the business for which the plan is being developed, the date on which it has been written, whether it is a first copy or a revision, and the name of the writer.

Policy and Philosophy Statements

Before serious planning can be undertaken, the framework and parameters for the plan must be established. General business philosophies and corporate policies which are relevant to a risk-management plan should be outlined. These might include, among others, staff qualifications, overall curriculum followed, industry-association standards, general safety policies, driving policies and guest-to-guide ratios.

These statements form the assumptions for the rest of the document and are carried forward to other documents such as trip plans, emergency-response plans and guide protocols.

Risk Analysis (1)

Specific hazards to the business are analysed. One section might include the identification of various objective and subjective hazards within the operating area, while an additional section would include specific risks to the business.

a. Identification of hazards

It is difficult to generalize about the types of risks to which an individual business might be exposed, because different locations, activities, guests and conditions give rise to different hazards. To reduce the likelihood of overlooking important hazards, risk managers approach hazard identification systematically, using tools that include an evaluation of expected activities in the business, hazard checklists, research into site-specific features, interviews with key personnel, site inspections to identify environmental and infrastructural hazards, and a review of incident history.

It is important to consider both business risks and program risks at this stage. Business risks may include such things as not finding insurance coverage, not receiving an expected permit, inability to find suitable staff, lack of cash flow and loss of market. Program risks are those generally associated with field activities, such as avalanches, drowning, rockfall, lost persons and hypothermia.

b. Evaluation of hazards

After a list of potential hazards has been created, it is important to evaluate them. The simplest method of doing this involves the risk manager using professional judgement to estimate the probability (frequency) and consequences (severity of loss) of each hazard's occurrence. Rather than ranking hazards in some order of importance, it is more appropriate to group them into general categories, as any hazard with the potential for a loss that would result in financial catastrophe for the business is similar to any other hazard with the same potential result. There are two primary criteria for evaluating hazards:

Frequency

The frequency of incidents for each hazard is the probability of their occurrence. Certain incidents, because of their possible frequency, will demand attention over others. Some incidents may be expected to occur on each trip, others once a year, and still others only once in the life of a business. *Frequency* may be clustered into the following three categories:

❖ *Often*
Incidents are expected to be recurring, happening more or less on a routine basis.

❖ *Occasional*
Incidents are infrequent.

❖ *Rare*
Incidents would be unusual and unexpected but not impossible.

Severity

The severity of an incident associated with a particular hazard measures the size of loss. Certain incidents, because they may entail more loss, will demand attention over others. Consideration must be given to both physical injury and organizational impact. Severity can be clustered into the following four categories, whose definitions may vary depending on the trip:

❖ *Severe*
Death or major injuries may occur, or the possible business losses are of such magnitude that the trip or the organization would not survive.

❖ *Moderate*
Substantial injuries that are not life-threatening may occur, or the magnitude of the losses would not be fatal to the trip or the organization but would have substantial consequences.

❖ *Minor*
The losses resulting from these hazards are injuries that would require attention but that could be dealt with using the existing resources on a specific trip or in the business.

❖ *None*
These hazards involve incidents that require no intervention or have no negative financial or other impact on the organization.

Based on these criteria, business managers or trip planners should assign a high, medium or low priority to each hazard and create strategies to mitigate the effects of these hazards. It may be helpful to use the following types of charts:

Table 9-1 ❖ Hazard-frequency Ratings

Hazard	Often	Occasional	Rare
Loss of insurance			X
Loss of permit			X
Drowning			X
Bear contact	X		
Axe injury			X
Burn		X	

Table 9-2 ❖ Hazard-severity Ratings

Hazard	Severe	Moderate	Minor	None
Loss of insurance	X			
Loss of permit	X			
Drowning	X			
Bear contact	X			
Axe injury		X		
Burn			X	

Table 9-3 ❖ Hazard-frequency/severity Matrix

	High Frequency	Low Frequency
High Severity	Bear Contact	Loss of Insurance Loss of Permit Drowning
Low Severity	Burn	Axe Injury

Risk-management Strategies

Once the hazards have been identified and evaluated and the ensuing level of risk identified, the next step is to implement specific risk-management strategies suitable to each hazard. This phase of the risk-management process primarily involves deciding which of the techniques available should be used to deal with a given risk. In making these decisions, the planner considers the size of the potential loss, its probability of occurrence, and the resources (financial, physical, human) available to meet the loss should it occur.

Risk management recognizes two broad approaches to dealing with the risks faced by a business or on a trip: *risk control* and *risk financing*. *(Please refer to Figure 8–1 on Page 102 for illustration.)*

Risk control

Risk control focuses on minimizing the risk of loss to which the business or trip is exposed. Techniques for risk control include, but are not limited to, *exposure avoidance* and *loss reduction*:

Exposure avoidance: Any decision taken by an organization to avoid or limit involvement in an activity with the intent of reducing risk to that organization constitutes exposure avoidance. An example is a business choosing not to include a certain activity as part of its programming in order to avoid the resulting risk. Similarly, the trip planner who due to potential risk chooses not to include a specific activity as part of a particular trip or who limits the number of times a specific activity is offered, is making an exposure-avoidance decision. In the example presented in the above charts, prohibiting axes on trips would be an avoidance decision.

Loss reduction: Loss reduction comprises those techniques aimed at preventing and/or reducing the severity of a potential incident. They may be preventative in nature or control-oriented and may consist of communication tools, educational tools, the removal of hazards that may cause accidents, or the elimination of "unsafe" acts. Examples are the application of signage for control, the use of pre-trip and pre-activity briefings, the presentation of safety talks, the implementation of increased instructor-participant ratios for high-hazard activities, the removal of an infrastructural or environmental hazard and forbidding guests and/or guides to participate in select activities. In the above charts, examples of reduction techniques would be to ensure that the guide instructed all guests in the proper use of an axe, to have the guide supervise its use and to have all axe users wear boots.

Risk Financing

Risk financing concentrates on financing the risks that remain after the application of risk-control techniques. Risk-financing techniques involve a choice between *risk retention* by the organization and *risk transfer* to other parties.

Risk retention: This is the retention by a planning organization of risk that cannot be prevented with risk-control techniques and is not transferred to others. Retention of risk may be carried out deliberately, unconsciously or as a result of the inability to transfer the risk. Any risk that is retained by the organization must be paid for by that organization in the event of loss. For instance, an organization that carries out an activity resulting in loss and that does not have adequate insurance coverage may be held accountable to pay for the rest of the losses itself.

Risk transfer to insurance: This is the transfer of specific financial risk to insurance as the result of losses specific to a particular hazard (fire, theft, medical, liability, etc.).

The amount covered by the policy is the amount of financial risk that is transferred to the insurer, while the deductible and any losses above the insured amount are retained by the organization.

Risk transfer through contract: This is the use of contracts to transfer the risk of certain types of losses to another party. This party may be another organization (such as a contracted business or guide) or a guest on the trip. Such contracts may include rental agreements, assumption-of-risk forms, legal releases, indemnifications, and employee or volunteer-worker contracts.

Risk transfer through volenti: This is the attempt to transfer the risk of certain types of losses to program participants by having them acknowledge that they are aware of the risks inherent in the activity, that they understand the scope and scale of these risks and that they agree to voluntarily assume the risks (voluntary assumption of risk). Any use of tools such as pre-trip information, educational material, legal releases, indemnifications, or warnings on tickets is an attempt to transfer financial risk to participants through *volenti*.

Incident-response Strategies

It is important that adventure businesses develop response strategies to address identified hazards. The implementation of the necessary strategies to deal with business risks becomes the responsibility of the business manager. All strategies need to be carried out far enough in advance to allow the business to continue to run smoothly. For example, last-minute attempts to arrange permits for trips creates the risk of interrupting business operations if a permit is not issued in a timely manner.

In addition to the risk-management plan, it is necessary to develop a trip plan for each trip, which includes trip-specific emergency-response strategies (*see the section below on trip plans*). It is important that the emergency-response strategies and policies developed in the risk-management plan provide structure for the trip plans that follow. For example, business policies regarding axe use on trips, driving policies, staffing ratios and the content of first-aid kits all provide direction for trip planners and leaders in their lower-level planning activities.

Organization, Roles and Responsibilities

An emergency-response structure that includes an organizational chart outlining appropriate lines of authority should be developed in the planning stage. The risk-management plan should identify specific individual roles: the person having full authority, the personnel responsible for remedial action, the chain of command, and on-scene authority for the organization. It is important to clarify prior to an incident the types of events which can be looked after by the guide, the point at which the business manager takes over, and the roles of various office staff in an emergency.

The plan should further identify the scope of each person's activities (what, where, when, how): how staff will keep each other informed, when outside authorities are to be contacted, what on-site actions are expected, etc. This helps keep personnel on task and also assists in keeping them within the bounds of their authority.

Flow charts or action checklists are valuable for condensing information and for enabling quick decision making during an incident. If checklists are used, they should contain sufficient detail to ensure that all crucial activities are covered and should be in a format that will be useful to personnel during an emergency.

Resources

Hazard identification and risk assessment assist in establishing the external and internal resources, personnel and equipment that might be needed in order to effectively respond to an emergency. All required resources should be identified, including quantities of equipment and supplies and their accessibility, and staging locations.

It is critical to determine the capabilities of various external response groups such as ambulance, police, fire and search-and-rescue teams, and lawyers and public-relations consultants. Clearly defined procedures should be written down that direct the mobilization of various resources during an emergency. Mid-event is not the time to be trying to find out who to call in order to get the necessary response. Much faster action will have to be taken.

Communication Systems

Planned, integrated and organized communication policies and systems are the key to successful emergency operations. Quick, accurate information is vital for the safe and efficient handling of all emergencies. Appropriate radio and telephone communications may need to be made available. During an emergency, the demand on communication systems can be enormous and additional radios and telephone lines may be necessary to implement a response.

Public Information

Accidents involving casualties will attract significant media attention. The objective is to have the event become a one-day story only and to avoid a continuing series of headlines and features dragged out over weeks. A public-relations or media plan of action should be developed which stipulates who will do media releases, when they will be done, what the guides in the field should do when they are approached by the media and how to prevent guests from talking to the media.

Emergency-response Activation

This section of the plan should describe the procedures for processing emergency calls. Regardless of the location of the emergency, the initiation procedures should indicate who is responsible for receiving the information and how it is to be channelled. The activation process should ensure that those persons in authority (key personnel) are alerted. Office staff need direction about what they should do and who they should call when they get an emergency call from a guide in the field.

Reporting

Emergencies should be reported to ensure public safety, comply with company policy and satisfy legal and insurance requirements. The plan should indicate who is responsible for such reporting and how, when and to whom reports are to be made. Parties that may need to receive reports include the company's owners, the police, the company's lawyer, the company's insurance broker and the insurance underwriter's lawyers.

Emergency Operations Centre

The emergency operations centre (EOC) becomes the focal point for coordinating the response operations during an emergency. For small events, the EOC functions may be represented by only one person and be located in the field or in the business' office. For larger events, it may be necessary for additional staff to be brought in, for consultants to be hired to assist with public relations, lawyers and insurance agents to be notified and for press releases to be issued. In some regions, the local search-and-rescue group may have resources and facilities available that can be helpful in managing a large-scale incident.

Site Security

Plans should identify the potential need for security. In an emergency, security may assist in preventing or minimizing personal injury by establishing and maintaining a security perimeter, reducing the exposure of people and assets, restoring normal operations as soon as possible and controlling the public and the media. The police will assist with this and can control road and trailhead access points, the accident site, and/or the airspace surrounding the site.

Contact Telephone List

A list of telephone numbers of any internal and external resources that could be of assistance during an emergency should be compiled prior to an event. This list should be reviewed each year and kept current.

Action Plan and Controls

In order to carry out risk-management planning, the manager needs to create an action plan that will ensure that risk-management strategies get implemented, and also evaluated for their effectiveness. The action plan should identify the risk-management strategies that are going to be used for each hazard and the person responsible for facilitating a particular strategy. It should also include a timeline for the completion of each item. In some cases, the manager responsible for the implementation of the overall action plan may be required to train staff in how to carry out their allocated tasks before these tasks can be completed.

Conducting Safety Reviews

A safety review is a process for assessing the safety status of an organization which involves a team of qualified people reviewing the standard operating procedures of an organization, providing feedback and making specific recommendations about safety matters. These reviews are sometimes also called peer reviews. Historically, they have been used more in the United States than in Canada, but they serve a very valid purpose.

There is likely no better process than a safety review for proving to a court that a business or organization has undergone an assessment by external personnel. The review results in a document, written by a group of experts, which clearly outlines where the organization meets, exceeds or falls short of the current industry standard. A safety review also provides an excellent demonstration of an organization's concern for safety matters and of its attempt to exercise due diligence in learning the standards.

The validity of a safety review largely depends on the qualifications of the team carrying it out. These individuals are potential witnesses in court, and their qualifications will speak volumes about the legitimacy of the process. In addition, of course, care must be taken to address any deficiencies identified in such a review as quickly as possible.

The review team's role vis-à-vis the host organization is intended to be one of helpful and constructive collaboration. The team members should serve as consultants to the program managers and should establish good communication with as many staff as possible in order to learn about the strengths and weaknesses of the organization. The reviewers need to observe an appropriate selection of activities so that they can gain a solid understanding of the program's operations.

A safety review is intended to be wide-ranging in its nature; however, the process typically looks at the following areas:

> ❖ client-screening techniques
> ❖ the program-admission process
> ❖ staff hiring, training and qualifications
> ❖ administration systems
> ❖ program activities
> ❖ emergency procedures
> ❖ logistics
> ❖ facilities
> ❖ transportation
> ❖ manuals, policies and procedures (2)

Trip Plans

Guides and program planners need to plan trips adequately and prepare for any associated emergencies. A written trip and emergency-response plan is often required. A well-conceived document will be useful in proposing the trip to a business, in preparing logistics and in providing the basis for pricing the trip. Knowledge about potential incidents and emergency-response options makes for a faster, better-prepared response.

Trip Description
This section consists of a description of the trip, including its location and a short narrative.

Itinerary and Time Plan
The description of the trip itinerary should indicate camping points, identify exit routes and analyse the terrain. It should present a clear time plan specifying travel times and the length of each day. The inclusion of a map of the route showing exit options is helpful.

Staffing Needs
This section should list the guide-to-guest ratio and the number of staff needed, as well as hiring qualifications and training requirements.

Clientele Suitability
This section provides a description of the type of clientele suitable for the trip — specifying age, sex, fitness requirements, experience levels, prior training, etc.

Instructional Progression
It is important to present material in a progressive manner. This section should outline how the program content and the trip itinerary will be progressive in nature and ensure that clients have the necessary knowledge, skills and abilities to continue taking part. If participants will be arriving without the appropriate experience for a remote or technical trip, the progression must take this into account.

Logistics
This section should indicate starting and ending points, times of departure and return, support-staff requirements (drivers, food preparation, etc.) and any special demands on the business' support services.

Equipment Requirements
This section provides lists of personal and group equipment that needs to be provided by the client and the organization. It should include lists for clothing, group equipment, and first-aid and repair kits.

Income and Expense Budget

If a trip plan is to be part of a proposal, an income and expense budget may be required, including a suggested list price.

Wrap-up

This section details the wrap-up elements that will be carried out, such as equipment clean-up and inventory, debriefings and reporting.

Evaluation

This section describes the evaluation processes that will be used after the trip. This may include safety and incident reports, guest-satisfaction surveys, and goal-attainment and profitability assessments.

Trip Policies

As a "lower-level" plan, any individual trip plan must carry forward the policies of the risk-management plan. These may include driving policies and guide-to-guest ratios. In addition, there may be policies specific to certain types of trips, such as rules that apply to isolated river trips, to the water levels at which a river can be paddled, or to the use of firearms in bear country.

Emergency-response Plan

An emergency-response plan is developed for each trip itinerary or activity category. This plan may be developed as part of a trip plan, or independently with the intent of applying it to individual trips or groups of trips. Some businesses prepare response plans for activity categories such as skiing, rock climbing, trail riding, etc., rather than for individual trips, while others prepare them trip by trip. Still other companies prepare emergency-response plans according to hazard grouping, where the specific location does not matter. For example, in a helicopter-skiing business a plan would be prepared for avalanches, falls into crevasses, helicopter crashes, lost skiers, parties stranded overnight, and the prevention of helicopter pick-ups due to bad weather.

The approach taken will depend on the business and will be influenced by the skills and expertise of the guides.

Hazard Identification and Risk Analysis

Hazard identification — as in the risk-management plan, but in this case specific to the trip — should identify both human-caused and natural factors that could pose a threat to people and property.

Risk analysis is a structured process that attempts to identify both the extent (severity) and likelihood (frequency) of potential events. It should answer several basic questions:

❖ What can go wrong on this trip?
❖ What are the effects and consequences of each potential incident?
❖ What is the likelihood of the incident happening on this trip?
❖ How often can the incident be expected to happen?

It is essential to identify the types of emergencies that have occurred in the area of operations, to determine which scenarios are plausible and to categorize them. Possible emergencies may include rockfall, drowning, burns, avalanche, lost persons, etc.

Impact Analysis

Impact (vulnerability or effect) analysis determines the potential effects of the hazard on personnel and/or the business should an accident occur. These analyses track the hazards from their source to potential areas of damage. The risk can be placed into categories of frequency (often, occasional or rare) and severity (severe, moderate, minor or none). Threats that receive a high rating in either or both categories require strategies to reduce their impact and plans to respond to any resulting accidents. Frequency and severity charts similar to those in the risk-management plan can be used here also (*see Page 113*).

Organizational Roles and Responsibilities

An organizational chart outlining decision-making responsibilities should be developed and should be consistent with the parameters outlined in the risk-management plan. The emergency-response plan should outline who is responsible for doing what in the case of an accident on the trip, when outside authorities should be called, what on-site actions should be taken and who can spend how much money.

Flow chart or action checklists are valuable for condensing information and helping individuals make decisions. If checklists are used, they should contain sufficient detail to ensure that all crucial activities are considered.

Resources

As in the risk-management plan, trip-specific hazard identification and risk assessment assists in defining which external and internal resources, in terms of both personnel and equipment, might be needed to deal with probable scenarios. It is important to identify all the resources required to effectively respond to an emergency on this specific trip, including accessibility and available quantities of supplies, maps, food, equipment, clothing and shelter.

It is also critical to determine the capabilities of various external response groups such as ambulance, police, fire and search-and-rescue teams, helicopters and other commercial operations in the trip area. Clearly defined procedures should be outlined regarding when and by whom the various outside resources will be mobilized.

Contact Telephone List

A list of the telephone numbers and radio frequencies of any internal and external resources should be compiled and maintained and made readily available at the business office. All guides in the field must carry the relevant numbers.

Notification

The scale of an incident should be determined from the initial information gathered. Some types of emergencies can be handled by the staff already in place at the site of the emergency. Other types of emergencies, which are beyond the capability of those at the scene, are likely to be considered major and to require additional resources, expertise and formal management. Once the required resources are determined, notification may need to be provided to the business office or to a separate incident-management site if there is one.

Emergency-response Activation

This section of the plan should describe the correct procedures for processing emergency calls. In the case of an accident in a remote area, there may be a significant lag time before the business manager is informed. Regardless of the location of the emergency, the initiation procedures should indicate how the guides are to relay the information and who is responsible for receiving it. The emergency must be accurately assessed in order to determine exactly the form of outside assistance required.

Resource Mobilization

Once key staff have been alerted and an initial assessment of the required personnel and equipment has been made, these resources should be assembled in an orderly and coordinated manner. The plan should designate the person responsible for mobilizing people and equipment. It should also identify appropriate spending authorities, relevant limitations and procedures and the respective responsibilities of the guide, the business manager and the business office.

Reporting

Emergencies may need to be reported to a number of parties in order to ensure public safety, satisfy legal or insurance requirements, comply with company policy and enable the timely capture of witness statements. Either the risk-management plan or the trip plan should indicate who is responsible for reporting, when and to whom reports are to be made and who is responsible for gathering and holding the reports.

Emergency Operations Centre

The emergency operations centre (EOC) becomes the focal point for the coordination of response operations during an emergency. It is necessary to clearly identify the EOC for each trip. It may be possible to generalize in the risk-management plan; however, if the trip takes place in an area far removed from the business office, it may be necessary to identify an EOC location closer to that area. For example, if a business based out of Boulder, Colorado, has an accident in Peru, a local, Peruvian-based response will obviously be required.

Emergency Protocols for Guides

Although field staff may be familiar with company policies and procedures regarding what is expected of them during an emergency, they should be provided with specific information that they can carry with them in the field. This is especially important for a business that hires a number of part-time or contract staff who may not have had the opportunity to become familiar with the business' risk-management philosophy, techniques and policies.

The following information is intended to give an example of the guidelines that a business can provide to its guides. The approach taken may vary according to the owner's interests, the philosophy of the company, and the guides' qualifications and their familiarity with the business.

Level of Response

While most businesses prefer to respond to emergencies in as self-contained a manner as possible, they recognize that there may be instances where outside assistance is required. Responses may be categorized into the following types:

✦ *Type-1 response*

This is a response to an accident that can be handled by the guides and personnel on site. The response is self-contained, using only the personnel and equipment within the group.

✦ *Type-2 response*

The assistance of additional personnel, and possibly a helicopter, is required.

✦ *Type-3 response*

Responding to the accident involves complications that call for external help (usually the assistance of organized responders).

✦ *Type-4 response*

This is the response to a fatality.

Response Protocols

It is anticipated that most injury evacuations will be of *Type 1*, where the guide(s) and guests on the scene are able to take care of both first-aid treatment and evacuation with the personnel and materials on hand. This type of incident should be reported to the business office on completion of the trip.

A *Type-2* injury evacuation requires additional personnel, and/or plane or helicopter assistance. Additional personnel may include other guides or guests from the business, or recreationists or guided groups in the vicinity. In this type of incident, the guide is expected to oversee first-aid treatment prior to evacuation. If a land-based evacuation is not suitable and an air evacuation is required, on-scene guides may authorize a government air evacuation. If this is not possible for some reason, or if it is an out-of-province or international trip, a commercial helicopter may be authorized by the guide. This type of incident should be reported to the business office at the earliest convenient time.

A *Type*-3 injury evacuation requires organized rescue responders such as National Park Service wardens, provincial-park rangers, or personnel from provincial emergency programs, provincial police, the local county sheriff's office or the Department of National Defense. On-scene guides may authorize the initiation of such services if deemed necessary. This type of incident should be reported to the business office as soon as possible.

Type-4 responses should be reported to the closest police detachment and the business office at the earliest possible time. The patient should not be moved from the accident site until this is authorized by the coroner's office or the police.

Communication with the Business Office

Communication with the business office regarding emergencies should take place on secure land lines if at all possible. Caution must be exercised when using non-secure communication means such as mobile radios, cellular phones and VHF or UHF radios. When attempting to communicate with the business office regarding emergency situations, guides should contact, in order, one of the following:

❖ the business manager
❖ the office manager
❖ the business owner
❖ another company guide

Guests should not be required to communicate with the business office regarding emergency situations, as this is the guide's responsibility.

Media or Public Interviews

Guides or guests of the business are expected to refrain from giving interviews or other information to any members of the media, the general public or the patient's family until such time as permission is given by the company. The business will designate a liaison person who has the responsibility of providing information regarding the incident to the media, the public and the patient's family. This will be done in conjunction with the on-scene guide.

In the event of an accident, guides must provide adequate client education and control in order to ensure that information is not given to outside interest groups.

Insurance

Guests are required to have adequate medical insurance coverage for the program activities. This usually involves a minimum of a provincial or state health-care plan for activities within the country.

For courses outside the country, guests are required to obtain medical coverage that is adequate for all the activities in which they will be involved. This coverage is confirmed with all guests by the business office prior to the trip's departure and does not need to be checked by the guide.

Records

On-scene guides are expected to gather and keep the following records in the event of an accident:

❖ a written log of the event, including times
❖ sketches and/or photos of the area and the event
❖ a record of all first-aid treatment provided
❖ witness statements from all guests on the trip
❖ witness statements from other recreationists in the area
❖ personal statement from all on-scene guides explaining the circumstances of the event

These records could be used to defend a legal action and should be written with this in mind.

Contact Numbers

Guides should carry telephone numbers and radio frequencies for all local resources and business contacts including the local police, relevant aircraft companies, the business office and the home phone numbers of the business staff.

Staff Manuals

The business needs a written staff manual in order to communicate its goals, philosophies and policies to its staff. A staff manual provides material on which to base staff training, ultimately reducing the training time required within the business and resulting in increased consistency among staff. Problems with personnel can often be attributed to staff having a lack of background knowledge about the business and an incomplete understanding of how they are to carry out their jobs. Although content will vary from company to company, the following list provides topics to consider in writing a staff manual:

Business and Staffing

❖ history of the business
❖ business goals and objectives
❖ the motivations of the business
❖ ownership structure of the business
❖ organizational chart
❖ reporting structure
❖ roles and responsibilities
  • administration
  • support services
  • guest familiarization
  • guides

❖ job descriptions
❖ remuneration policies
❖ benefits
❖ work schedule
❖ leaves
❖ expectations of staff
  • appearance
  • professionalism
  • behaviour
  • interpersonal
  • problem solving
  • technical

continued

Operational Guidelines
- geographic areas of operation
- activities of operation
- provincial and federal regulations
- public relations

- equipment, food, garbage, water and human-waste procedures
- transportation guidelines
- insurance regulations

Program
- company philosophy on risk and safety
- standard of care expected
- client description and customer-care needs
- legal liability
- accident prevention and the role of staff
- equipment inspection
- guest safety orientation
- first-aid treatment procedures
- waiver-form procedures
- medical-form procedures
- incident-reporting procedures

- trip plans
- emergency-response plans and protocols
- safety-talk procedures
- contents of guide's pack and first-aid kit
- trip evaluations
- post-accident strategies
- dealing with an injured guest
- dealing with the group
- dealing with the family
- dealing with the media
- forms and reports

Safety Talks, by Will Leverette

One of the most common allegations in a lawsuit is that the business failed to warn and inform participants of the inherent dangers in an activity and to give adequate instructions in what to do and how to do it. Before guests engage in a particular adventure activity, guides should provide a safety talk that educates participants about that activity, includes warnings and discusses proper technique and equipment use. The business may choose to have guides carry a safety-talk outline similar to the following:

Safety Talk Outline
Introduction
Give the safety talk at the initial staging area early in the day. Introduce yourself and other staff. Tell the guests to listen and think, and make sure that they hear the talk. Stress that responsibility for safety is shared by the participants. Explain that the activities involve inherent risk and that guests must understand the nature of these risks. Acknowledge that your trip cannot be totally risk-free. Treat the group as your witnesses and do not allow a group member to be absent for any part of the talk.

Activity Specifics
- ✧ Introduce the area and outline the weather to be encountered and what can be expected on the trip.
- ✧ Describe the inherent dangers such as hypothermia, cold water, rockfall, twisted ankles and avalanches.
- ✧ Explain proper equipment use.
- ✧ Demonstrate proper technique (sit like this, paddle like this, etc.).
- ✧ Explain to the guests what they should do in the event of an emergency (how to get back on the raft, the role of the safety kayaker, what to do if they get lost, etc.).
- ✧ Stress the importance of following instructor/guide directions at all times.

Participant Responsibility
- ✧ Explain the level of physical involvement.
- ✧ Confirm that no one has a medical or physical condition that would preclude his or her participation.
- ✧ Explain that no drugs or alcohol are to be consumed prior to or during the activity.
- ✧ Ask the guests to notify the guides if they notice any problems with the equipment and to report any incidents or accidents.

Closing
- ✧ Ensure that everyone has signed a release form.
- ✧ Ask if there are any additional questions.
- ✧ Arrive at a consensus with the guests that they understand and accept what is entailed by the activity.
- ✧ Provide an out for participants who do not want to participate; their participation should be voluntary.

Notes to Chapter Nine

1. Parks Canada describes a very similar risk-analysis format in its *Visitor Risk Management Handbook*, December 1994.
2. Some of this information is taken from the unpublished *Safety Review Manual* by Ian Wade and Mike Fischesser for Outward Bound U.S.A., 1988, revised 1995.

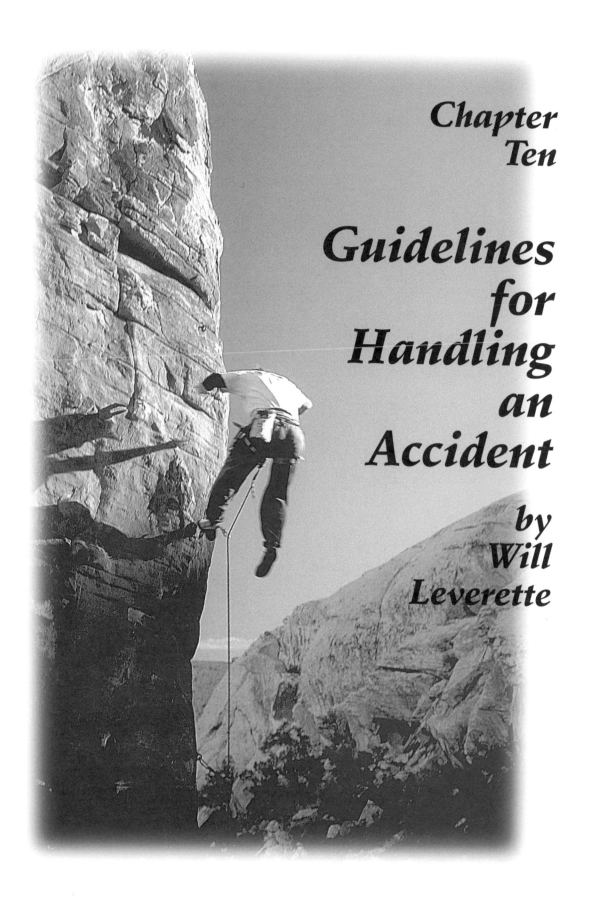

Chapter Ten

Guidelines for Handling an Accident

by Will Leverette

Often, the opportunity for a business to defend itself against frivolous litigation is lost in the few days after an accident occurs. As time goes by, memories fade, details are forgotten and the opportunity to put a professional face on the entire incident is lost. Quite often, litigation attorneys wait until the statute of limitations has almost expired before they file a lawsuit. Their hope — which is unfortunately only too often based on reality — is that by the time the lawsuit is filed so much has been lost and forgotten that it becomes impossible and impractical for the business to defend itself. The sooner a business gathers information concerning an accident, the better its chances of effecting a positive outcome if faced with a lawsuit.

The following guidelines will help the concerned business manager handle accident situations properly and avoid this type of litigation. It is critical to keep in mind that speed is of the essence. Any delay can end up costing the business, and ultimately the industry, thousands of dollars in legal fees and higher insurance premiums.

Relationship to the Injured

Lawsuits are initiated by injured parties when they feel that the business has not demonstrated the highest level of concern for their well-being and personal safety. Care and concern towards all guests must start before an accident occurs and should be ongoing elements throughout any trip. Learning people's names, responding to them as individuals and showing concern for their well-being right from the start is probably as important as, if not more important than, the care and concern shown to participants once the accident has taken place. Remember to make friends; friends are less likely to sue.

Search-and-rescue experts and psychologists have taught us that an injured person responds better and develop lesser degrees of shock if one individual is assigned to the patient, stays with the person throughout the evacuation, rides with them in the ambulance or other vehicle to the hospital and checks them in, remains with them in the waiting room and gives them the same kind of care and attention that a parent would give his or her own child. This consistent thread from the accident site through the evacuation and into the hospital has a calming and settling effect on accident victims and is often the most important factor in discouraging them from going into litigation. It is critical that any accident victim not be given an opportunity to get upset.

The comfort and the psychological well-being of the rest of the participants are also important factors. Family members, witnesses and other individuals are going to be canvassed later for their opinions regarding events and the type of care given to the injured party. These people can, in certain situations, become accident victims themselves because of their own mental state and a business' disregard for their well-being. It is important to make certain that the entire party is taken care of, administered to and made comfortable. Their evaluation of what occurred will be a critical element in any litigation process.

What Guides Should Do

Do not make guarantees of a speedy evacuation. You can say that you are doing the best you can, that you have sent for help, that the group is in a remote situation and that it could take some time to get out.

Do not make any admission of guilt or wrongdoing, such as "We've had problems here before," or "This horse has been a problem for us in the past." Comments of this nature will be very damaging in litigation. Do not make value judgements or statements concerning what happened. It is okay to say that you're sorry the client is hurt and that you are doing everything you can to ensure as speedy an evacuation as possible, and to show empathy and sympathy for what the patient is experiencing.

Begin taking field notes regarding the accident as soon as possible. It is vital to first answer the following basic questions: What happened? Where did it happen? When did it happen? Who was involved in the accident? As early as possible, look at your watch to determine the time of the injury and the time of the evacuation, and make notes concerning the details of what happened. You might also begin to take notes of things that were said — witness statements, injured-party statements and family-member statements — concerning how and why the accident occurred.

The Full, Written Report

Everything that is recorded and written from the moment of the accident until the insurance company's attorney begins to direct the investigation is considered "discoverable". The litigating attorney can request and obtain any and all discoverable records and use them in the litigation process. It is therefore essential in all written records concerning the accident that managers and guides avoid comments that could be damaging later on. Comments that admit guilt, cast blame or are judgemental or accusatory in nature are to be strictly avoided. Stick to the facts. The simplest and easiest rule to follow in writing up an accident report is to answer the question "What happened?" Avoid opinions, assumptions, personal feelings, and evaluations made during the height of emotional turmoil that often follows an accident.

* Use an incident/accident report form as an outline for collecting and developing the report. Answer all questions as completely as possible and make certain that all handwriting is readable.
* Encourage each guide to develop his or her own written account of what happened, using as basic guidelines "What happened?" "Where did it happen?" "When did it happen?" and "Who did it happen to?"
* Never address the "why" of what happened in writing.
* Accidents with known injurious consequences involving evacuations and transportation to medical personnel for further evaluation and treatment should be reported to the business' insurance company within 72 hours.

Concerning Witnesses

Get as many people who witnessed the accident as possible to fill out a "witness statement" as soon as possible. If practical, get the injured person to fill one out, too. If not practical, mail the patient a form. Present the form to witnesses and victims as a trade-association tool, used to gather information on accident trends, which will be used to help prevent similar accidents, if possible, in the future. Do not portray the process as an insurance-company requirement. If practical, tape-record the statements.

A lack of time may prevent you from taking witness statements; sometimes the very best you can do is to simply ask witnesses what happened. Write down what they say. Comments such as "The injured person would not have been injured if he had been more careful," "The injured person refused first-aid or treatment," or "The injured person contributed to the accident through her own actions," are extremely important.

Unfortunately, given time, witnesses and injured persons often change their versions of what happened. The sooner you obtain a record of their impressions of the events that led up to the accident and that immediately followed it, the more likely you are to get an accurate picture of what actually happened.

Photographs

Obtain as many photographs as possible of the accident site and the victim. With any kind of luck, someone on the trip will have a camera. Pay particular attention to the terrain encountered by the accident victim immediately before the accident occurred. As well, canvas all participants to see if by chance someone might have recorded the actual accident on film. Video footage could be extremely useful.

Communication with the Media

If there has been a fatality, even the prudent business can count on some contact with the news media. Often this contact leads to poorly documented facts about the accident and results in bad publicity and potential litigation problems. The company owner should designate a spokesperson to provide information to the media. This person should do the following:

- ❖ Prepare a factual statement to be reviewed by legal counsel if necessary.
- ❖ Communicate the statement to wire services such as AP and UPI.
- ❖ Set up a system for handling telephone inquiries.
- ❖ Remember that the job of the media is to sell press. In the event that the media have picked up on the accident and arrive at the scene, they may try to sensationalize the story as much as possible. Reporters may ask leading questions, make accusatory statements and heckle members of the guided party or press them for statements concerning the events of the accident. These statements may or may not be accurate. At the scene of the accident and/or the

evacuation, it is best to appoint a representative to speak to the press and to advise this person to make very few statements.

❖ Have the guide encourage anybody from the media to contact the main office for a further statement. The guide's best defense is to say, "We do not have any comments or statements at this time." Media representatives must be kept away from all members of the party if at all possible.

You will find the news media co-operative if you deal with them straightforwardly and with the facts — subject only to legal constraints, consideration for next-of-kin, protection of the injured and good taste. Any hesitation or impropriety in dealing with the media in an emergency situation not only may escalate their news coverage but in the long run can also be critically costly to your program and take a great deal of time to remedy. From a public-relations point of view, the objective is to have a one-day story and to avoid a continuing series of headlines and features dragged out over a period of days or weeks.

Most dealings with the media will take place over the phone. Rather than reading a "canned story" to the caller, the spokesperson should have a written list of key points for reference and should tell the story in his or her own words. The press will want to know the following:

❖ What happened.
❖ Where it happened.
❖ When it happened.
❖ The names of the people involved.
❖ Why it happened.
❖ Background on the adventure activity.

The spokesperson should provide an accurate and full disclosure of the facts and co-operate to every extent possible with the media.

When information cannot be released, explain why. For example, if next-of-kin have not yet been notified, doctors' orders prohibit interviews of survivors, etc. Withholding the names of victims pending notification of next-of-kin is appropriate and will be respected by the press. However, do not deny the occurrence of the accident itself.

Refrain from speculation: when you answer an inquiry and the answer is not known, state that it is not known. Make certain that all media representatives have equal access to information. Upon discovering that erroneous information has been given to the media, provide correct information as soon as possible. When a reporter prints or broadcasts erroneous information, inform the reporter, not his or her superior, and provide the correct information.

It is imperative that no one, including the spokesperson, release any information that identifies the responsibility for the accident without first consulting legal counsel. Specific problems arise when any of the following occurs:

❖ Assignment of fault, or criticism of conduct, policy or equipment is made public without a full explanation of the circumstances of the accident, which should be developed through a complete investigative process.

❖ Information regarding the nature of the injury or illness is released prior to diagnosis by a licensed medical physician.

❖ Names of victims are revealed prior to notification of next-of-kin.

Follow-up

Again, it is essential that a representative from the business make visits or phone calls to the injured person concerning his or her welfare. If personal attention, care and concern are demonstrated, the victim will be less likely to sue. Remember that everything you say or do before, during and after the accident may be scrutinized in detail, either by litigating attorneys or in a court of law.

Any equipment that was involved in the accident or that could conceivably have contributed to it should be pulled out of the regular equipment inventory and kept secured in a separate place for future examination. Photographs and equipment-use logs can also be helpful.

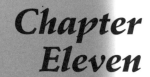

Chapter Eleven

Risk Management: An International Perspective

by Daniel Garvey

*I*f an organization had a catastrophic incident involving the serious injury or the death of one or more participants in a foreign country, would it know what to do? What should be done at the moment of the incident? What steps must be taken after the immediate crisis is over? This chapter focuses on the unique risks and safety challenges of conducting adventure programming in foreign countries. It examines some of the policies and practices that might be considered when adventure-tourism businesses operate internationally.

The term "international" is a relative concept depending on one's country of origin. Although not country-specific, the recommendations in this chapter apply to most businesses regardless of the home country or foreign programming site.

Any international crisis (incident/accident) can be viewed from three overlapping perspectives: before the crisis, during the crisis and after the crisis.

Before the Crisis

Naturally, the best way to reduce emergencies in a program is to minimize the possibility of an accident happening in the first place. When a program takes place in an international arena, prior planning is even more critical than it might be for domestic programs, where staff can be expected to understand the culture within which they are working. Listed below are a few cautions, somewhat unique to international programming, that need to be considered before clients set foot in another country.

Be aware of making assumptions about the country being visited

The single most important way to prevent and manage incidents is to be aware of the assumptions being made in another cultural setting which are based on experiences in the organization's home country. Most organizations offering international adventure activities have conducted similar activities in their home country. The procedures and practices used to reduce risk and handle emergencies in the home country have been developed to meet the needs of that particular country. As the organization expands to the international arena, many of the expectations about how emergencies will be handled must be reexamined. Often the difficulties experienced while trying to manage an international medical/safety incident can be traced to faulty assumptions.

For example, just because a vehicle that looks exactly like an ambulance arrives at the scene of an accident, one cannot assume that the injured person is being taken to anything that resembles a hospital. In some countries, ambulances roam the streets looking for people who may be injured. Once the injured party is in the ambulance, he or she may be transported to a private "clinic". This clinic may be the bottom floor of someone's house or a building similar to a garage outside the house. The level of medical care one can expect to receive in such a clinic can be marginal at best.

Other examples of assumptions that can cause problems are the assumptions that basic medicines are available throughout the world and that if available they can be purchased.

In some countries, or regions within countries, medicine may not be sold to people even if they are sick, have the money and are accompanied by a doctor. The policy of that country may be "Medicine is for local people, not foreigners."

In every decision, carefully examine the cultural blind spots that may be present. As trips are planned, review and eliminate as many assumptions as possible. Invite professionals from the foreign country to examine the organization's protocols and procedures for reducing risks and handling emergencies in that country. Organize mock emergencies where staff can list the assumptions they are making about how the incident might unfold. Place these mock incidents in several cultural settings in order to enable staff to see how certain expectations may be difficult to guarantee. Checking assumptions and practising how to respond in different cultures will reduce the number of unanticipated problems that will arise during the resolution of an incident.

Carefully evaluate the risks associated with in-country travel

One of the biggest concerns that must be considered in international programming is the potential risk to participants and staff as they move from point to point in-country. The business needs to evaluate the relative danger of various modes of transportation — i.e. bus, train, plane, taxi and car. Pre-trip decisions should be made to reduce the in-country transportation risk to participants and staff. The unique safety concerns of each country to be visited must be evaluated.

Assessing the relative risks of different modes of travel in a foreign country can be difficult. In-country agents or contact people associated with the trip may not be of much help in assessing the relative safety risks of travel in their country since they may not perceive the dangers of certain modes of transport in the same way as would staff from the home country. Also, some agents make money by using certain carriers and use them regardless of their safety records.

Travel advisories and cautions issued by the home-country government may be helpful. There are excellent travel-advisory Web sites available. Also, speaking with representatives from agencies and companies that have been doing business in a particular foreign country may give some information about well-known risky activities or locations.

The following are a few examples to illustrate the importance of gaining an awareness of the particular travel dangers in a foreign country: Those firms doing business in Kenya need to be aware that the road between Mombassa (on the coast) and Nairobi (in the interior) is exceptionally dangerous and should not be travelled at night. Likewise, there has been a taxi war going on in parts of South Africa. Patrons who ride a small minivan in a city could be in jeopardy if the driver attempts to take the van into an area of that city served by another van company. Motorized rickshaws in many developing countries — India, for example — are exceptionally dangerous. Riding in a motorized rickshaw may provide a great in-country experience, but the injury cost could be very high.

Pre-planning, and establishing transportation policies for the business are the most important steps in minimizing travel problems. If the business is reasonably aware of the travel concerns in a certain country, plans can be made before the group arrives to avoid high-risk travel activities. Without prior planning and established policies to follow, a leader who is responsible for transporting a group of participants within the foreign country may make a poor decision because of having become insensitive to the objective safety concerns of certain local travel options. It is important for businesses to gain a good awareness of the recommended travel precautions for each country in which they operate and to adjust their practices accordingly.

In addition to choosing the safest mode of travel, guiding staff must be prepared to be assertive with hired drivers in other countries. Many travellers want to understand and embrace local customs; although this attitude is desirable in most cross-cultural encounters, it must be cautiously applied to the driving behaviour of some hired drivers. When groups travel by bus or car, guides must be firm about the quality of driving that is expected. Telling a driver "Slow down!" or "Be more careful!" is a difficult thing to do in another country, but it is certainly true that leaders and their groups may be in greater danger if nothing is said.

Create an emergency evacuation plan

Prepare ahead of time for the possibility of an evacuation from the country. Which airlines serve the relevant foreign airports? Do these carriers have a policy about removing seats from planes in order to transport injured persons back home?

In most regions of the world, there are evacuation services that will fly in, stabilize the situation and airlift the injured person(s) to the nearest first-rate hospital. The contact numbers of these services should be carried by the in-country staff and should also be on file at the home office. These services are very expensive, often costing thousands of dollars per participant; however, many insurance companies will cover this cost.

Determine how costs associated with emergency medical care will be paid

Who will make the decision regarding an evacuation should one be required? If time is a critical element, as it usually is, will the parents or spouse be contacted before the decision to evacuate is made? Will the participant's insurance company be contacted to see if it will cover high-cost evacuations? What will it pay for? What if the accident occurs on a weekend or holiday when the insurance agent is unavailable? There must be a protocol in place to handle such emergency-related issues.

Another possible solution for medical problems that occur in a foreign country is to assemble medical help from the home country and send it to the scene. In a situation where the injured party is in a hospital or clinic in a foreign country and the quality of care in that country is unacceptable, it may be best to send the required medical help to the site rather than move the injured participant(s). Again, a bit of pre-planning will greatly facilitate the resolution of any such emergency.

Know the availability of medical prescriptions in foreign countries

Before the group arrives, determine the availability of prescription drugs in that country. Local embassies will have information about the availability and relative costs of prescription drugs. Making the assumption that prescriptions will be readily available can create problems for the participants and the business. In Japan, for example, a foreigner seeking to obtain drugs may be told, "These drugs are for Japanese people." In some developing countries, the shelf life of drugs may have expired, so always check the dates. In other countries, it may be very difficult to get any prescription drugs. If a particular illness or parasite is prevalent in-country, be sure to antic-ipate how the program will obtain the appropriate drugs if needed. One recommendation is to bring along on a trip all the medications required to stabilize and transport a participant to an adequate medical facility. Consult with the program's medical resources to determine which drugs should be chosen. Paying for drugs can also be a problem. In some foreign countries, credit cards and traveller's cheques cannot be used to purchase prescriptions or to obtain med-ical services, and the local currency may be the only form of tender acceptable.

Know the locations and emergency-response capacities of embassies and other similar institutions

Before any group arrives in a foreign country, find out what medical support is available at the home country's embassy in that country:

* ✤ Does the embassy have a doctor on staff? What role do the embassy staff expect to play in the case of a serious emergency?
* ✤ In a case involving a serious injury or accident, would the embassy doctor attend to the medical needs of those injured during the emergency?
* ✤ Would the embassy doctor provide aftercare and ongoing treatment? In some countries, the embassy doctor will take over as a primary-care physician. In other countries, the doctor may simply provide a list of phone numbers of recommended medical staff in the area.
* ✤ In addition to the embassy, what other governmental and non-governmental organizations are operating in the foreign country (i.e. military bases, compa-nies and agencies)?

Contact should be made with these resources before sending trips into the foreign country. In addition to providing important information about local travel, these contacts may be useful in the unlikely event of a program emergency. The level of support and help may vary greatly depending on the staff at a particular embassy. In some offices, the staff will be very helpful and supportive of the business needs. In other instances, the embassy staff may be hard to find and difficult to work with. Gain as much information as possible about embassies and other foreign contacts before sending a trip to an area. Also, monitor any changes in embassy staff leadership, as this can affect the service delivered.

Know each country's communication systems

Program field staff should be familiar with the communication systems in each country to be visited. In general, the newer the telecommunications technology available in a foreign country, the more dependable the service. In other words, e-mail is better than fax and fax is usually better than phone. This may seem self-evident, but many programs still rely on the telephone during emergencies because the in-country staff is unsure about where to locate e-mail or a fax machine. Make sure that program staff know the telecommunications capabilities of the country being visited before they arrive. In some parts of the world, it may be nearly impossible to use a phone reliably; however, the fax or e-mail systems may work very well. Carrying a satellite telephone on a trip may alleviate all of the in-country communication problems, as this removes the need to rely on local technology.

Have back-up procedures in place in case communication breaks down between the in-country staff and the home office. Different strategies exist for staying in contact with staff in foreign countries, so be prepared to use alternate approaches. In 1991, a group of American program participants was in Moscow waiting to depart via plane. Unrest in Moscow resulted in the government shutting down the airport and the phone system. The group was out of contact with the home office for a number of days. Alternatives for staying in contact with this group could have been used — for example, contacting the U.S. news companies that continued to broadcast from Moscow and having messages delivered and collected via those agencies.

Create and publish clear procedures for families of participants in case of emergencies

If a serious incident occurs, international news services will begin to investigate and run the story. The home office will be deluged with calls from family and friends seeking information about program participants. Businesses should devise systems to help families of participants access the organization to get accurate, timely information. Develop and enforce very clear instructions for staff to follow when dealing with family and friends, and attempt to establish one contact person for them within the business.

Generally, the only interaction a program will have with the family and friends of a participant is in the case of a crisis. The reputation of the business is important. Also, the manner in which the family is treated while an incident is being handled will be a significant factor in determining whether they choose to sue a program afterwards.

Conduct proactive participant briefings

The more informed the participants are about the safety issues associated with foreign travel, the more they can manage their own personal behaviour. A participant is more likely to get hurt while approaching or leaving the adventure experience than while participating in the program. Time needs to be spent prior to a trip instructing participants about the safety issues of mountain travel. Local customs should also be explained ahead of time. For example, the hand gesture that people in North America might use to signify "OK!" is an offensive gesture in Brazil, similar to giving someone "the finger".

Participants should receive verbal and written information about the risks associated with travel and behaviour in the country that they will be visiting. There should also be regularly scheduled "briefings" so that updated information can be shared with clients.

During the Crisis

Provide adequate and appropriate staff support

Hire good staff to place in the field and use the resources of the home office to support them. Unless there is a compelling reason to do otherwise, create the expectation that the home office will do what is requested by the in-country field staff who are handling the crisis. It is very difficult to manage all the complexities of an incident in another country from an office in the business' home country. Assumptions made in the home office regarding the best solution to a problem may be irrelevant to the situation faced by the field staff member. In one incident in Istanbul, a young woman had not returned to the trip from a party she was attending with a local man. Large quantities of U.S. cigarettes were purchased for the police who were helping to locate the woman. A request by the field staff to "pay off" the police may have seemed inappropriate in the home culture; at the time, however, this request was an honourable demonstration of appreciation for the work that the police were doing. Needless requirements that in-country staff check in with the home office, or disagreements about the appropriate course of action may delay the response to an emergency and increase the possibility of greater harm to participants. Hire good staff and trust their judgement; they should be the in-country experts.

Prepare field staff to expect the participation of senior business staff in the resolution of the emergency

Once an accident has occurred, although the in-country field staff may be doing everything they can to handle the situation, the home-office staff are often anxious to be supportive and to help manage the crisis also. The separate needs and goals of the in-country staff and the home office staff create the potential for a clash at a time when the entire organization should be working at a highly effective level. The potential clash between these two staff groups needs to be anticipated. Before an accident occurs, in-country staff should be trained to expect the quick arrival of senior staff members immediately following an incident. Explain to them that a visit from the home office is not a negative reflection of their competence but rather a sign of support.

Senior home-office staff should be dispatched to the emergency site as soon as possible following the incident. They usually have more organizational experience and are aware of the various capabilities and contacts available to the business to help resolve the crisis. In addition, the arrival of the home-office staff elevates the importance of the incident within the culture of the business — demonstrating to staff, participants, family, and the public in general that the organization takes the incident very seriously.

During a crisis, in-country staff should continue in their roles as trip leaders and attempt to meet the needs of the other group participants. The home-office staff should coordinate and solve the problems caused by the incident. A brief discussion about how the larger organization responds during a crisis will reduce the discomfort between the person(s) on the scene and the newly arriving senior staff member(s) when an actual incident occurs.

Designate senior-level staff to respond to the emergency, but use the business manager sparingly. Some managers will want to be the point person on all major issues. Be careful about the time the manager spends talking to families and responding to their needs. Family contact is very important, but the overall leadership of the organization is also critical. The manager often needs to remain focused on the culture of the entire organization as it responds to the incident. Any manager who becomes overly identified with the family has the potential to be consumed by their problems and is rendered less effective regarding larger organizational needs. A senior-level administrator or a lead guide, who can access the resources of the organization, is usually the best person to coordinate the response efforts. In some organizations, an emergency-response team is selected to handle unforeseen problems.

Attend to the physical and emotional needs of other group members, including the field staff. In the general area of support, try to do whatever can be done to help the group members who are on the trip. Let them call home, eat more food, have a rest day — whatever they need at the time. The long-term strategy for dealing with post-traumatic stress will be more successful if the organization makes its resources fully available to the participants. Despite the fact that trip leaders and the home office are often interested in regaining a sense of normalcy, it is advisable to resist the tendency to get busy immediately following a significant incident. If participants are encouraged to finish the trip without fully discussing and gaining a sense of understanding about the incident, they may create their own view of what happened without the benefit of other group members' perspectives. They should be helped to create a shared understanding of what happened and why. When time is not set aside for participants and staff to create a shared vision, multiple versions of the incident often develop. This may be unsettling for the participants and can create additional difficulties for the program long after the incident.

Carefully monitor and reevaluate the assumptions being made by staff as they attempt to resolve the crisis

It is critically important to be careful about one's assumptions not only before but also during an emergency in a foreign country. For example, in some countries emergency personnel who arrive at the scene of an accident involving head and neck trauma may not have a neck brace or backboard.

While in the midst of an emergency, be aware of everyone's location at all times. In most areas of the world, there can be several hospitals in one city. It is easy, in the confusion of the incident, for injured participants to be transported to different medical facilities. Once transport has been arranged, take particular care to understand where the patient is being taken.

Make sure that you know how to say and spell the name of the medical facility; in countries where the alphabet is unfamiliar, have the name written down in the local language.

Also, when a participant is taken to a hospital or clinic, be careful about your expectations regarding the level of care available at this institution. In India, for example, adequate medical help may be provided but no food or water is given to patients. These will have to be provided by company staff.

Be clear and decisive while taking action

When dealing with emergency situations, seek advice and guidance, then act with clarity and confidence. During an international incident, many different groups may seek to give advice and influence the decisions being made, including guides, business owners, embassy personnel, the families of participants and the members of boards of directors. Strong, direct leadership will help focus all of these various elements and harness their resources in the service of those in-country who are dealing with the incident.

After the Immediate Crisis

Tend to the needs of families and friends

In the case of a death, family members will often try to get as much information and memorabilia as possible concerning their loved ones. Ask participants and staff to save any photos showing the deceased prior to the accident. Written reflections about the deceased will also be greatly appreciated. Encourage participants to be in contact with the family.

If a participant is hurt and hospitalized in a foreign country, family and friends may need a great deal of guidance and support if they decide to make the trip to be with the patient. Assist families in obtaining visas, air tickets and emergency passports if needed. In the case of a death, help family and friends who are interested in visiting the site of the accident to make travel reservations using the organization's travel agency. Also use the organization's resources to support the efforts of family and friends who are interested in helping participants following an incident.

Take appropriate steps to reduce any confusion, irritability, depression, fear and postponed anger following the emergency

Significant incidents leave their marks on people. Each individual will respond to the incident differently. In one case, it took several weeks before a participant could admit that he hated one of the other clients because that person had failed to help him at the time of the accident. Postponed emotional outbursts may be especially common from staff who have been too busy meeting the needs of the participants and fulfilling their organizational duties to fully assimilate recent events. The random nature of significant accidents is hard to handle for certain staff and participants. Some people will turn this confusion outward and become angry and hostile. Others will turn their confusion inward and begin to manifest signs of depression or unreasonably fearful behaviour. In all circumstances, the program should anticipate that it might take a long time for a serious incident to be understood by participants, families, friends and staff and to become part of the organization's history.

Obtain competent legal advice

As soon as possible, an attorney should be consulted to advise the business regarding possible legal issues that may result from the incident. It is important to remember that attorneys are hired for advice not program decisions. The business has relationships with guests, families and friends which must be recognized in all its decisions. The role of the attorney is to protect the business' interests once the business has decided on a particular course of action.

A business faced with the aftermath of a significant incident should maintain open and honest communication with all relevant parties. If the "golden rule" has any application, it certainly is a great concept for dealing with tragedy. Members of the business should treat people as they themselves would want to be treated if the accident involved them or members of their families.

Conduct both internal and external program reviews

Any incident, whether major or minor, provides an opportunity for the organization to re-examine its policies and procedures. Internal and external reviews will enable a serious focus on the factors that contributed to the incident and will identify steps aimed at reducing the chance of such an accident reoccurring.

An internal review allows the business to look at its policies and practices and to establish whether they were thoroughly applied in the case of the incident. An external review is carried out by a group of professionals who are outside the organization. Their responsibility is to evaluate both the soundness of the organization's policies and the way in which staff in the field follow these policies. The external review team will evaluate the policies and practices in the organization according to the standards of care within the industry as a whole.

Anticipate the difficult questions that follow emergencies

Regardless of how well an organization was prepared, how well the crisis was managed and how well the business responded afterwards, criticism will follow any significant incident. This criticism is a positive thing in many ways because it causes organizations to take responsibility for errors in judgement which may have contributed to the incident. Staff need to be prepared for this evaluation and possible criticism, even though they may have done a remarkable job in reducing any further danger and in treating the participants affected by the incident. Staff who are prepared and briefed for this difficult process of questioning will deal with it more effectively and may be able to avoid internalizing guilt and responsibility that is not rightfully theirs.

Conclusion

Despite the cautions outlined in this chapter, international travel offerings are tremendously valuable components in the product mix of many adventure-tourism businesses. Incidents, however, can and do happen. The trick is to be as prepared as possible before beginning international programming. Where lack of preparation is minor, it can lead to inconveniences such as missing a train or running out of money. Where lack of preparation is significant, it can put participants at risk.

When an incident occurs in a foreign country, uneducated assumptions and hopes about how things will be resolved are inadequate. International programming demands policies and practices that recognize the cultural realities of the countries in which the business intends to operate.

This chapter was originally published as an article in The Journal of Experiential Education, *21, 2 (August 1998).*

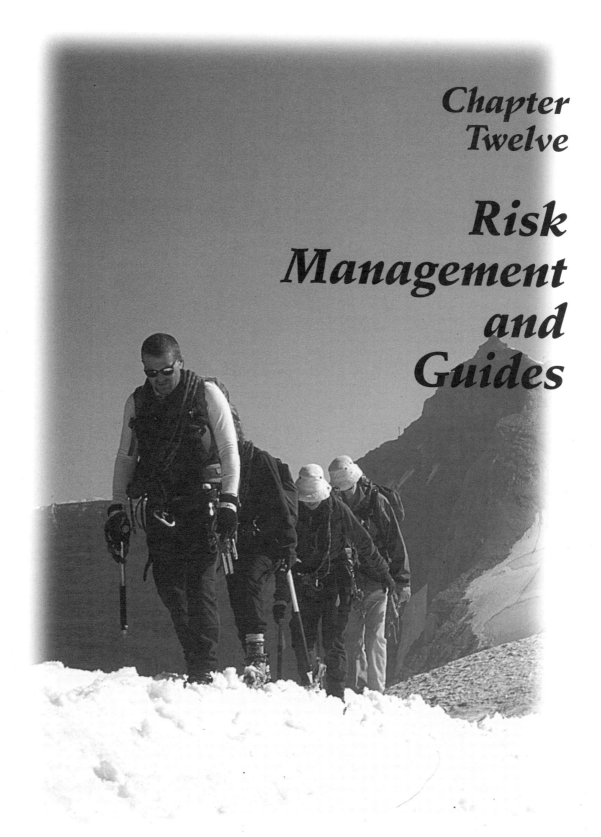

Chapter Twelve

Risk Management and Guides

A large portion of a guide's role — the assessment of hazard and the minimizing of risk — falls within the domain of risk management. The guide's job is a complex balance: to expertly build experiences that bring participants safely into a high-risk environment they may not be accustomed to, while at the same time planning and providing for their care in the case of a disastrous event.

Old-school guides had a tendency to train hard at becoming technically proficient in a technical activity while giving less consideration to managing risks and to response planning. Risk management consisted of preparing for trips as well as possible and throwing in a first-aid course or two just in case. Things are different now, with career-oriented guides striving to be as professional as possible and as well rounded as necessary. Today, guides routinely carry out rescues, write emergency-response plans, accompany injured guests to hospitals, counsel guests about inherent risks, provide safety talks, issue waivers and deal with victims' families. It has become a much more complex industry to work in, and the level of responsibility accepted by guides is increasing every day.

Recognizing and Avoiding Hazards

Guides have always been trained to recognize and avoid the hazards of the activities they lead, (1) including developing the knowledge and experience to avoid the hazards inherent in the wilderness environment. They must be able to competently analyse which hazards are real and to instinctively make decisions to avoid those hazards. For example, businesses rely on suitable training programs and voluminous field experience to develop the ability of a ski guide to recognize avalanche microterrain and to pick suitable route lines through it. This is called terrain assessment and route finding.

Managing Hazards

Guides apply a wide variety of group- and environment-management techniques that are intended to minimize guests' exposure to risk. This is much more complex than just being able to identify environmental hazards and to pick appropriate routes. It also deals with the way the group is managed, the smoothness of the line, the comfort of guests in a harsh environment, the degree of control in which the trip is carried out, and the extent of the knowledge margin above what is minimally required to deal with the hazards.

A guided group that pinballs through hazardous terrain without consequence is by no means as safe a group as one that is clearly in control on a safer route throughout — even if neither has an incident. One group is benefiting from good luck, and the other from good management. Thus, a ski guide with a high level of snow-science training will make a safer guide than one without that same level of training — if only because he or she understands what the other does not, ultimately creating a higher margin of safety.

It is important for guides to inform their clients about the risks inherent in an activity.

In order for clients to voluntarily assume any responsibility for accidents, they must have an appreciation for potential accidents and their seriousness.

Guides voluntarily expose themselves and their clients to some measure of risk — this is a natural part of achieving reasonable objectives and undertaking appropriate challenges. Deciding if voluntary exposure is appropriate requires forethought, active decision making and constant evaluation. Guides and clients must accept that they have a measure of control over exposure to hazards: they need not go into the mountain environment. On the other hand, once they choose to expose themselves to hazards by entering the mountains, they must accept that there is only so much that even the most experienced guide can do to control hazards. To some extent, luck and chance are normal, acceptable factors in any mountain activity — this must be understood and accepted. (2)

Managing Emergency Situations

When an accident happens and a guide is in the vicinity, there is an immediate tendency to rely on the guide for expert knowledge. As a professional, the guide is somewhat expected by the public and the courts to respond. However, although the guide has a duty to respond in the case of an accident to his or her client, there is no legal duty to respond in the case of an injury to a non-client. Nonetheless, some professional associations do have codes of conduct that require the guide to respond to incidents involving non-clients.

It is reasonable for a client to expect that a guide, and the business he or she works for, will provide a timely and expert response to an emergency. This means that guides should be trained in emergency response — including first aid, incident command and organization, priority decision making, and company policies.

When an emergency occurs, the guide must be able to:
* ✤ stop and think
* ✤ take charge
* ✤ stabilize the situation
* ✤ eliminate further hazard
* ✤ consider the options
* ✤ reach the patient
* ✤ stabilize the patient
* ✤ package the patient
* ✤ evacuate the patient
* ✤ keep a log
* ✤ care for the remainder of the group
* ✤ gather witness statements
* ✤ deal with outside agencies

❖ handle the media

After the incident, the guide may need to be able to:

❖ gather records
❖ debrief the incident with the remainder of the group
❖ counsel the remainder of the group
❖ deal with a victim's family
❖ provide statements to insurance-company lawyers
❖ maintain composure with an upset boss and an accusing industry

Feelings of personal grief and responsibility will be strong, and many guides leave their jobs and the industry after losing a client in a fatal incident.

Developing a Guide's Philosophy of Rescue

Nowhere is a professional attitude on the part of the guide more important than in an emergency situation. There are many demands at the site of an accident; in order for actions to be effective and efficient, they must be preplanned as much as possible.

Professional rescuers take the following view of emergency response: "The professional rescuer is not engaged in emergency work. Rather he or she is engaged in a series of premeditated series of actions intended to alleviate the suffering and/or hazard experienced by another person. For the professional rescuer this is a normal, day-to-day activity." (3) The professional guide, like the professional rescuer, must understand the conceptual difference between carrying out a methodical, routine response to some other person's predicament and engaging in an irregular response to events that he or she does not expect. In the first case, the guide understands and accepts that he or she will be involved in responding to accidents over the length of his or her career and that a response should be professional, pre-planned, consistent and in control. The second case is the symptom of someone who is surprised that the risks hypothesized about in adventure activities are real and who is faced with being in charge of an accident while being unsure of what to do. The difference between the two approaches is defined as professionalism.

Professional rescuers and guides work from a philosophical perspective. They need to know what to do in the event of an emergency and be ready to act. They need to stop, think and make a plan before reacting. Rescuers and guides realize that they may deal with emergency prevention and response over and over again in their careers. They know that heroism is an unacceptable attribute in a rescuer but that compassion is desirable. They know that response priorities must include the rescuer and other clients in addition to the injured party, and that exposure of additional clients is not acceptable.

The professional guide, placed in an emergency-response role, needs to be able to adopt a police, fire and ambulance professional's approach to the task at hand. This takes a while to achieve, but the alternative amounts to the guide accepting only the good part of the job — without the bad.

The Guide's Role in Risk Management

The guide plays an important role in the risk management of a business. He or she makes day-to-day decisions regarding exposure avoidance, loss prevention, loss reduction, risk transfer and risk retention.

Exposure Avoidance

Guides make exposure-avoidance decisions whenever they decide not to engage in an activity. Examples are the ski guide who makes the decision not to ski a specific slope, the canoe guide who has a group portage around a particular rapid and the rock-climbing guide who does not let a client lead-climb a certain route.

In making such a decision, the guide is evaluating the readiness of an individual or group to undertake the risk involved in a specific hazard. This is an expert decision that requires foresight and acute judgement, skills that develop over time.

Loss Prevention

Guides make loss-prevention decisions whenever they decide to reduce the frequency of participation in any activity. Examples are the ski guide who decides to take a group down a certain section of terrain quickly and who does not allow clients to repeat it, the sea-kayak guide who only does one open-water crossing on a trip and the guide who determines to do only one high-risk, technically difficult trip in a season. These guides are all making decisions regarding how often they will expose clients (and themselves) to a specific hazard.

Loss Reduction

Guides make loss-reduction decisions whenever they attempt to reduce the potential severity of a possible accident. Examples are the ski group that crosses a potential avalanche slope one skier at a time and the whitewater instructor who places a person with a throw bag at the bottom of a rapid or who allows only one kayaker at a time to paddle a section of river.

Risk Transfer — Clients

Guides make risk-transfer decisions whenever they warn and educate their clients about specific risks inherent in an activity. The canoe guide who provides formal instruction and warnings about the dangers of cutting firewood with an axe is attempting to prevent an accident but also to make people responsible for their actions if they do get injured. The climbing guide who provides good pre-course information, adopts a style of warning clients about specific risks and asks clients to accept them is attempting to educate participants and have them share the risks inherent in climbing.

Risk Transfer — Insurance

Guides make risk-transfer decisions whenever they choose to take out insurance policies for rescue, evacuation or liability. They have decided that if there is an accident requiring rescue or evacuation, they will not pay for the evacuation but will transfer this responsibility to an insurance firm who will pay these costs. The same applies to lawsuits; guides may determine to transfer the risk of loss to a willing recipient — an insurance underwriter.

Risk Retention

Guides make risk-retention decisions every day they work. The wilderness environment holds a wide variety of risks. On the whole, guides are aware of these risks — and their consequences. In the end, after all attempts have been made to reduce the severity and frequency of accidents, there is still a real risk that incidents will happen because the wilderness is an unpredictable environment. The risk that remains after applying skillful risk-management techniques is retained or absorbed by the guide and the business.

Lawsuits and Guides

Not all accidents are the responsibility of the guide. Nor are all accidents the result of negligence. In fact, the vast majority of accidents in adventure activities are the result of risks inherent in the activities and not the result of any mismanagement on the part of the guide. It is easy but irrelevant to second-guess and judge incidents after the fact:

> There can be no doubt that the determination of what constitutes an unreasonably high risk must be in the eyes of a reasonably competent heli-ski guide. And perhaps most importantly, the approach as to what constitutes a reasonable or unreasonable risk in any given circumstance from the point of view of a reasonably competent heli-ski guide must not be ascertained in hindsight. (4)

Guides will almost always be named in a lawsuit. Lawsuits are very stressful periods for guides. Feelings of personal grief and responsibility can be intense. It is a shame that many guides leave their jobs and the industry after experiencing a fatality in a group for which they are responsible; most doctors do not quit their practices after losing their first patient. It is my observation that guides are thus affected for the following reasons:
> ✢ Guides do not know what to expect beforehand.
> ✢ Guides accept excessive responsibility for what is, in most cases, a joint sharing of risk with the client.
> ✢ Feeling responsible for an accident is a serious blow to the ego and confidence of the guide (in a highly egocentric, competency-based business).
> ✢ Guides have not previously come to grips with the fact that adventure has inherent risk and that they are likely to see the result firsthand at some point in their careers.
> ✢ Businesses have a tendency to blame the guides for their misfortunes.

❖ The feelings of the guides are sometimes deemed expendable in relation to the defense strategies of the insurance company.

❖ There is little or no professional support or knowledge available in most adventure businesses regarding vital stress counselling for staff after a critical incident.

The Contracted Guide

One of the original intents behind hiring an independent contractor rather than hiring an employee may be risk-management based, i.e. to transfer the responsibility of an incident to the contractor. However, if a guide is an independent contractor, the business' insurance may not apply to the guide. It is probably in the best interests of the business' insurance company to "embrace" contract guides, bring them into the fold and defend them as part of the company's overall defense strategy. This may be advisable for a business so that it does not run the risk of having contractors take a position against it in court. Most businesses will do this.

Nonetheless, there is a possibility that the contractor will have to indemnify the insurance company for any losses paid out because of his or her actions. Many contract-for-service documents include an indemnification clause similar to the following:

> The Contractor shall indemnify and save harmless the Company from and against all losses, claims, damages, actions, causes of action, cost and expenses that the Company may sustain, incur, suffer or be put to by reason of any act or omission of the Contractor or of any servant, agent or subcontractor of the Contractor.

In the event of being named in a lawsuit, it is likely that independent contractor guides will require their own lawyers to look after their own interests. In order to afford this, most guides will probably need to have arranged their own insurance coverage.

Defense Strategy, the Insurance Company and the Guide

An insurance policy will state that the insurance company has the right to defend an incident as it sees fit, to make the defense decisions and to assign its lawyers to the case. Many business owners do not realize that it will not be they themselves who decide on defense strategy and that the insurance company will do this on the business' behalf. This may leave the business and its guides feeling a little empty at the end of the case — depending on their opinion of the defense applied.

One possibility is an out-of-court settlement. An insurance company may decide to make a payment offer to the plaintiff because this is deemed the cheapest or least difficult way out of the case or because it does not think the business will win in court. This may leave the guide with implied blame, as there will be no court ruling stating otherwise. Most lawsuits never get to court.

Lack of Insurance

Even today, many adventure businesses do not carry liability-insurance coverage. This information is not always provided to the guide, even when the guide asks. Because the guide will normally be named in a lawsuit, this situation would leave the guide paying for his or her own defense. Costs can also include a financial judgement because apportionment may be applied, leaving the guide responsible for at least part of the settlement. This is particularly a problem for guides who work for a variety of organizations during a season; contracts are often on short notice and for a short time period, and all the relevant questions regarding such things as insurance may not get asked every time.

Legal Fees

It is possible that a guide will need his or her own lawyer, even though he or she is covered by an employer's insurance policy. The business' or the insurance company's interests are not always the guide's best interests. This legal advice will cost money, and even a few thousand dollars is too much for many guides to pay. Without insurance, the guide may not be able to afford legal advice — a very untenable position in which to find oneself.

Risk-management Rules for Guides

❖ Always carry out due diligence in your risk-control obligations in the field. Do the best job that you can, to industry standards, and develop a reputation for being safe.

❖ Get as much accident-prevention, hazard-assessment and emergency-response training as possible. Take the training from reputable organizations that will make good witnesses in court on your behalf.

❖ Carry out a timely and competent response in the field.

❖ Keep good records in the field.

❖ Know if you are an employee or contractor.

❖ If you are a contractor, make sure you are listed on the business' waiver.

❖ If you are a contractor, know what the contract means.

❖ Know what kind of financial risk you retain with your job or your contract. Did you sign any indemnifications?

❖ Know the rules of workers' compensation.

❖ Be familiar with your own tort lawyer.

❖ Be as sophisticated as the business you work for in your understanding of such things as insurance, employment law and waivers.

Notes to Chapter Twelve

1. Some of the concepts in this chapter are taken from the *Rope Rescue Manual* produced by the Justice Institute of British Columbia (1990). The original version of this manual was written by Ross Cloutier.
2. Association of Canadian Mountain Guides, *Technical Handbook for Professional Mountain Guides* (1998), 5–4.
3. This is not original, but the source is unknown.
4. Madam Justice Koenigsberg in *Ochoa v. Canadian Mountain Holidays Inc.* (September 25, 1996), Vancouver C922041 (B.C.S.C.).

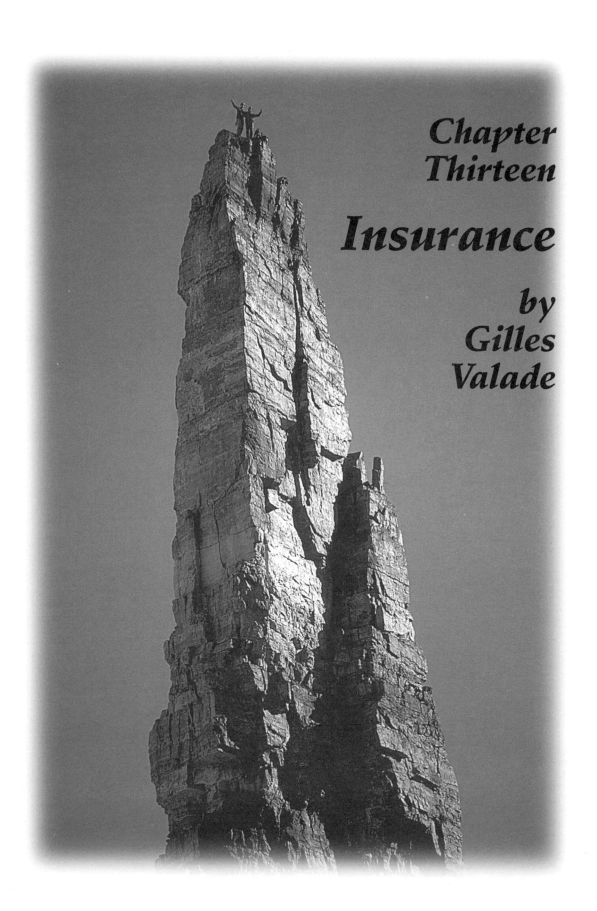

Chapter Thirteen

Insurance

by
Gilles
Valade

Introduction

*A*nyone involved in the delivery of adventure activities will sooner or later be confronted with the insurance issue. This might mean being involved in searching for insurance, purchasing insurance or dealing with an insurance claim. For many, it will prove to be a challenging and sometimes frustrating experience. Insurance is one of the most important and most common risk-management tools available (almost everyone has purchased some form of insurance at some point in time); yet insurance is misunderstood, is not a popular purchase and is usually bought more out of fear than desire. (1) The Insurance Institute of Canada mentions that many customers do not understand what insurance really is, what it is not, how rates are determined and how those rates are influenced by the marketplace. Additionally, many consumers do not understand the claim process and have grossly inaccurate ideas about the profitability of insurance companies. (2) This chapter attempts to shed some light on the insurance world as it relates to adventure-tourism operations.

Insurance — The Big Picture (3)

Most citizens generally benefit from three types of insurance products:

❖ *Social insurance:* This usually refers to programs offered by the state and includes medical plans, unemployment insurance and workers' compensation. In some jurisdictions, these insurance products may also be offered by private insurance companies.

❖ *Life and health insurance:* These insurance products are associated with a person's health or life and usually cover the financial risks associated with the loss of life or loss of income arising from death, sickness and/or physical disability as well as many other related causes.

❖ *Property and casualty insurance:* This is commonly referred to as "general insurance" and refers to any insurance product that does not fall under social or life insurance. Property and casualty insurance products include automobile insurance, residential- and commercial-property insurance, liability insurance and business-interruption insurance, among dozens of other insurance products.

In Canada, property and casualty insurance products are provided primarily by private insurance companies. A few provincial governments are involved in providing certain products. This is true for British Columbia, Saskatchewan, Manitoba and Quebec, where the provincial governments are involved in providing some form of automobile insurance coverage. Adventure operators are primarily concerned with property and casualty insurance products; this chapter will therefore examine only these products and their related issues.

Figure 13-1 ❖ Percentage of total premium by type of business in $ millions in 1997 (5)

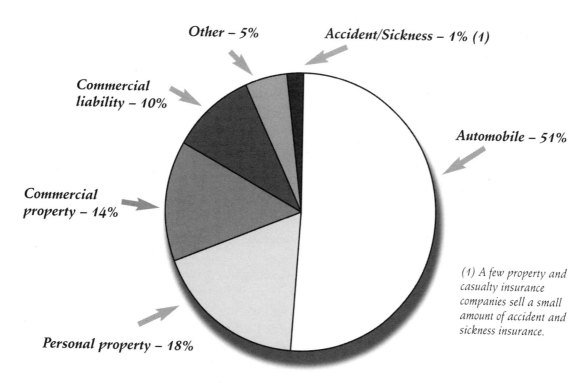

(1) A few property and casualty insurance companies sell a small amount of accident and sickness insurance.

The Property and Casualty Insurance Industry in Canada (4)

Over 230 private insurance companies offer property and casualty products in Canada. In 1997, these companies had combined sales of over $18.4 billion. In the insurance world, sales refer to premiums collected from the sale of insurance products. In addition, the total sales generated by provincial-government insurance programs generated $3.1 billion in 1997. The property and casualty insurance industry creates employment for approximately 100,000 people in Canada. *Figure 13–1* shows the sales breakdown by type of property and casualty insurance product.

The Players and Their Roles (6)

Much like any other product, the insurance product is available through a marketplace. In the property and casualty (P&C) industry, the main players involved in this marketplace are the following:

The Insured

The insured is the consumer purchasing the insurance and can be an individual, a society, a corporation or any other form of legal entity. The insured is the reason the other players exist. The adventure-tourism business is considered an insured.

The Intermediary

The intermediary is the link between the insured and the insurer (the insurance company). Usually known as the insurance broker or the insurance agent, the intermediary is the sales arm of the industry and shares the customer-service function with the insurer. The agent or broker is essentially supposed to identify the needs of the insured and match those needs with the products available from insurers. The intermediaries also collect the premium, provide ongoing service throughout the coverage period and become involved in the claim process if there is one.

   ✤ *The insurance broker:* The broker usually represents a number of insurance companies. Brokers are often regrouped in one business called a brokerage firm, which is generally able to respond to most of the insurance needs of a consumer, although there are exceptions. Some brokerage firms specialize in offering insurance coverage for certain types of businesses. Adventure-tourism operators are most likely to purchase their insurance through a broker who specializes in this type of business. Brokers are remunerated through a commission that is calculated as a percentage of the insurance premium collected from the clients. Commission rates vary from one type of insurance to another and even from one insurance contract to another. They can range from as low as 0% to as high as 25%. For example, if an operator's liability-insurance premium is $5,000 and the commission rate is 15%, the broker will collect the $5,000 from the operator, keep 15% ($750) and remit the rest ($4250) to the insurance company. The commission is generally included in the premium, but some brokers will also charge service fees over and above the premium. These service fees are not charged by the insurance company.

   ✤ *The insurance agent:* The insurance agent usually represents only one insurer and is generally involved in non-commercial P&C insurance. In most cases, the client belongs to the insurer not the agent. Agents may work on a commission or salary basis, or a combination of both. Adventure operators are most likely to purchase their P&C insurance through an insurance broker rather than an agent.

The Insurer

Commonly known as the insurance company, the insurer is the risk taker, the product designer (the insurer determines the insurance policy's coverage and conditions) and the payer of claims. It is the company providing the actual insurance coverage. Insurers can be divided into the following types:

❖ *Government insurers:* These usually take the form of government departments or Crown corporations and provide the following products: automobile insurance (where applicable), workers' compensation coverage and provincial medical plans, as well as other social-insurance programs.

❖ *Private insurers:* Most of the insurers in Canada are private corporations that can either be provincially or federally incorporated. Generally, private insurers sell their products through insurance brokers and agents, although some sell directly to the public.

❖ *Captive insurers:* These insurers are also private corporations, but with one main difference. They are usually created and owned by large commercial organizations or associations in an attempt to reduce insurance costs or, in many cases, because certain types of insurance are unavailable or difficult to acquire.

❖ *Other types of insurers:* These include co-operative insurance companies that are owned by their policy holders.

The Re-insurer

Re-insurers are companies that provide insurance coverage for insurance companies. They are the least well known of the players but one of the most important. Insurance companies need to get insurance themselves in order to spread their risks, just as a consumer does when purchasing regular insurance. The re-insurer is the risk taker that further spreads the risks and smoothes out wide fluctuations.

The re-insurance process works much like the regular insurance process. The insurer will offer its business to the re-insurer, who will decide whether or not to accept it. Having decided to accept it, the re-insurer will negotiate the terms and the premium with the insurer. There are twenty or so reinsurance companies doing business in Canada, although most of them are large international organizations. Re-insurers play a crucial role in the overall worldwide insurance industry. In recent years, they have been helping insurance companies share the claims associated with major natural disasters.

The Regulators

The regulators are the guardians of the public interest. In Canada, the P&C insurance companies are supervised and regulated by the federal and provincial governments. The federal Office of the Superintendent of Financial Institutions is concerned with federally registered and foreign insurance companies. The Provincial Superintendents of Insurance are concerned with insurance companies with provincial charters. The regulators ensure that insurance companies will be able to fulfill their financial obligations, that insurance contracts are fair and that business is conducted for the good of the general public. Regulators also supervise intermediaries and re-insurers.

The Dynamics of the Insurance Marketplace (7)

The insurance world may seem quite complex, and a better understanding of its functions would likely improve its image in the eyes of consumers. In order to objectively understand the property and casualty insurance industry, one must first understand its overall process, and the factors that influence this industry over a long period of time. This process can be compared to that of the stock markets; many factors are responsible for the rise and fall of stock prices, and it would be short-sighted to try and assess the stock market as a whole based on one event or on a short period of time. Similarly, many factors influence the make-up and pricing of insurance products in Canada. A few of the major influences are examined below.

The Marketplace

Insurance prices are influenced by the relationship between supply and demand. When supply exceeds demand, competition increases, prices are driven down and contract terms are less restrictive. On the other hand, when demand exceeds supply, prices increase and contract terms become more restrictive.

The marketplace forces are such that in certain circumstances, insurance prices go down even when claims costs are going up. In the insurance world, supply is determined by the volume of premium (sales) that an insurer is allowed to have in relation to its equity (financial strength). The greater an insurer's equity, the more premiums it is allowed to collect. Government regulators determine the ratio of equity to premium that insurers are allowed to maintain.

For example: In 1991, the P&C industry's equity was evaluated at $11 billion. A predetermined premium-equity ratio of 2.5 provided for a capacity of $27.5 billion. Since premiums in 1991 totalled $14 billion, the market was operating at only 52% capacity. This type of oversupply leads to extreme competition, price cutting and weakened underwriting. Underwriting is the process of evaluating a risk (an insured) and establishing the appropriate premium and conditions for that risk; this is generally done by the insurer.

On the other hand, a lack of surplus would have the opposite effect. The total capacity of insurers to write premiums could become less than the actual size of the market, leading to higher premiums and more restrictive terms. The same situation occurs in any industry when there is more demand for a product or service than there is supply.

The Pricing Process

Pricing is one of the more disputed insurance topics. Most people do not understand how premiums are established and why they vary from year to year. Insurance pricing is quite imprecise and is based on statistical data and probabilities. Insurance companies use past statistical data to price today's products in order to pay for tomorrow's claims. For example: Could insurers have predicted the "ice storm" of 1998? And could they have predicted that it would be three times as expensive as the Calgary hailstorm of 1991, which until then held the record for the most expensive insurance claim in Canada?

The pricing of insurance products can be problematic because of the following factors: (8)
- ✤ For many classes of business, the available statistical data is neither large nor homogeneous and therefore lacks the level of credibility required to produce premium rates with precision. This is especially true for adventure tourism and commercial outdoor recreation, for which there is very little statistical data available to insurers.
- ✤ Actuarial science is as much an art as it is a science. It often calls for informed judgements in lieu of hard statistics.
- ✤ Most importantly perhaps, the law of supply and demand reigns supreme in the marketplace. Marketplace forces overwhelm the pricing advice of the actuaries (the specialists who estimate future claims and premiums) no matter how credible the data or how elaborate the calculations.

The Impact of Fragmentation

In Canada in 1992, only 26 insurers had enough premium to achieve a 1% market share. There is no dominant force or pace setter, and there are too many insurers competing for a limited market. This leads to intense competition and a lack of price discipline; price becomes more a function of competition and market share than of the actual risk insured.

The Cost of Claims

It is normal to expect that insurance premiums will be directly influenced by the cost of claims. In reality, the manner in which premiums respond to changes in claim costs is somewhat complex and unexpected. For example, Conn and Van Zyl (1999) illustrate that, even though the claims experience of the P&C market is deteriorating, insurers continue to slash already low premiums. "Deteriorating claims experience" refers to the increased cost of claims and to decreased revenues due to lower insurance premiums. Insurers are prioritizing market share over profitability.

Insurance Cycles

The P&C insurance market is infamous for its cycles. Until the 1970s, the general pattern was three profitable years followed by three unprofitable years. But this changed in the '80s, when less profitable periods lasted longer and profitable periods were shorter. A few factors help fuel these cycles. First, when insurers become profitable, they also increase their capacity to sell more insurance, which encourages them to decrease their premiums in order to increase their market share. This reduction in prices will then result in less profitable years, which will decrease the insurers' capacity to sell insurance and thus lead to an increase in premiums. Another factor is the lag time between an increase in claims costs and the response in increased premiums; the insurers' reaction to increased claims cost seems to be delayed. One of the more famous P&C cycles is the liability crisis of the mid-1980s. This cycle was due to a combination of many factors such as decreased capacity, increased claims costs and an escalation of large court settlements. This cycle was intense and short-lived but had a lasting impact. This particular cycle hit the adventure-tourism industry quite hard, as operators and their activities were seen as potentially leading to court settlements.

Profitability

Another highly debated issue is the profitability of P&C insurers. The public's impression is that P&C insurance companies are highly profitable businesses, whereas the owners of P&C corporations would argue the opposite and say that insurers can barely make ends meet. The reality probably lies somewhere in between.

Insurers earn most of their revenues through the collection of premiums and incur expenses through the payment of claims and through operational expenses (employee salaries, rent, mortgages, utilities, etc.). The difference between these revenues and expenses is called the underwriting profit or underwriting loss (the profit or loss generated by the business of insurance). Insurers also earn revenues through investment income (investing the premiums of clients in order to earn income). (9) For every year since 1978, the P&C insurance industry in Canada has posted an underwriting loss (*see Figure 2*). Although individual insurers may have posted underwriting profits, the industry as a whole has lost money with the business of insurance. These underwriting losses have been offset by investment gains, which can vary widely from year to year depending on interest rates and bond/stock markets. (10)

In 1997, the Canadian P&C insurance industry posted a $469-million underwriting loss but posted an investment gain of $3.3 billion. The fact that insurers make most of their profits from investments fuels the theory that, in times of high interest rates, insurers will underwrite any kind of risk at any premium simply in order to have funds to invest. This behaviour has been called "cash-flow underwriting". Furthermore, cash-flow underwriting has been held responsible for fuelling many of the insurance cycles and their ensuing crises. According to the cash-flow-underwriting theory, insurers are more concerned with obtaining money to invest than with taking risks at levels that are adequate — in order to have more cash flow through the system. According to the P&C insurers, however, this is not the reality. The insurers say that in times of high interest rates and higher profits, the capacity of insurers increases (*see "The Marketplace" above*), which increases competition and lowers premiums. Additionally, more competitors will enter the marketplace when interest rates and the possibility of profits are higher, further increasing overall competition, decreasing rates and starting another cycle. If one combines years of high interest rates, increased competition and low premiums followed by a significant decrease in interest rates, a dramatic increase in large court settlements and a reduction in profits and thus capacity, the result is the mid-1980s insurance crisis.

Summary

As is any other industry, the property and casualty insurance industry in Canada is subject to

Figure 13–2 ❖ Underwriting and Investment Income in Millions of Dollars (11)

Year	Underwriting Loss	Investment Gain
1984	(917)	1,255
1985	(1,260	1,350
1986	(555)	1,509
1987	(541)	1,706
1988	(837)	1,945
1989	(1,520)	2,325
1990	(1,375)	2,378
1991	(1,584)	2,564
1992	(1,532)	2,521
1993	(1,506)	2,688
1994	(1,145)	2,074
1995	(703)	2,524
1996	(576)	3,131
1997	(469)	3,345

the forces of a marketplace and is therefore affected by supply and demand. The insurance-buying public does not fully understand this concept as it applies to the insurance product and finds it hard to comprehend the fact that premiums go down when claim costs go up and vice versa. This lack of understanding leads to the impression that the insurance-pricing process is totally improvised and disorganized.

Insurance is usually associated with negative emotions since it is a product that only becomes tangible when tragedy strikes (accidents, fires, lawsuits). Nonetheless, those who make an effort to fully understand the particularities of the insurance marketplace may benefit from a competitive advantage. (12)

Insurance: Definition, Purpose and Principles

Insurance can be defined as a method of sharing the losses of a few individuals among the many members of a group. A more formal definition as outlined in the *Insurance Act of Ontario* mentions that insurance is "the undertaking by one person to indemnify another against a loss or liability for loss in respect of a certain risk or peril to which the object of the insurance may be exposed, or to pay a sum of money or other thing of value upon the happening of a certain event". (13)

Insurance can also be viewed as a method of spreading risks. The adventure operator purchases insurance as a means of transferring certain business risks (such as legal liability) to an insurance company, who will in return spread this risk amongst the many other clients who have purchased insurance and thus provided funds for future claims.

The Basic Principles of Insurance

The first principle is that the premiums of the many will pay the losses of a few. This is the risk-sharing and risk-spreading process. The second is that the premium will be commensurate with the risk. This is the fairness principle, whereby the insured business contributes money to the pool (via its insurance premium) according to the likelihood that the business will cause a loss to the pool. (14)

What Insurance Is Not

In insurance, the term "to indemnify" means to put back in the same financial position as just prior to the loss. (15) This means that no gains should be made from an insurance claim. If an insured loses a 12-inch black-and-white television set in a fire, he or she should expect to be compensated for such an item but should not expect a larger or a colour television set. Insurance is not an investment with an expected return.

Summary

Insurance is a mechanism for preventing financial disaster and preserving peace of mind.

The Insurance Contract

The insurance policy is often dealt with trivially and regarded as a collage of incomprehensible clauses written (read "hidden") in fine print. In reality, however, the insurance policy is the document that provides evidence of a contract between an insured and an insurer. Insurance policies are therefore governed by the same rules that govern contracts in general, meaning that both parties receive benefits and have certain obligations. For insurance purposes, a contract means a contract of insurance and includes a policy; a certificate; an interim receipt; a renewal receipt or writing evidencing the contract, whether sealed or not; and a binding oral agreement. (16) Because of the particular nature of insurance contracts, however, the law makes three additional requirements: (17)

> ✦ **There must be an insurable interest**
> This means that an insured can only obtain an insurance contract for something that has the potential to cause him or her a financial prejudice. For example, you cannot get insurance for someone else's house unless you hold the mortgage to that house, in which case you have an insurable interest.
> ✦ **There must be a risk, and a promise of indemnity**
> The insurance contract is purchased to protect the insured against the possibil-

ity of a loss (risk). If a loss occurs, it is expected that the insured will be returned to the same financial position as prior to the loss, and this without profit. This is called the principle of indemnity. Without the requirement of indemnity, insureds would be tempted to profit from insurance.

❖ *An insurance contract is a contract* **uberrima fides**, *or of the utmost good faith (18)*

Because the insured knows more about the material facts of his or her own particular situation than does the insurer, he or she is in a position of greater knowledge. The law therefore imposes a duty on the insured to disclose any material facts, i.e. information that would influence a prudent underwriter in setting the premium or determining whether to accept or reject the insurance application. (19)

Insureds often do not appreciate that failure to disclose material facts, known as *non-disclosure*, (20) can have serious consequences. Non-disclosure can be an intentional or non-intentional omition of material facts. An insurer can render an insurance policy partially or totally void if there is non-disclosure on the part of the insured. In most cases, the insurer will invoke non-disclosure when a claim arises and unknown material facts are discovered. For example: An insurer has provided liability-insurance coverage to a canoe-tripping operator based on the knowledge that all the trips are on flat water, but the insured has failed to mention that a short section of white water between two lakes is part of the itineraries. The insurer can render the policy void and/or refuse to pay a claim, based on the fact that coverage would not have been provided had it been known that white water was involved. The duty to disclose material facts starts with the negotiation and application process and continues throughout the policy period. This means that the insured must inform the insurer as soon as he or she becomes aware of new material facts or as soon as his or her situation changes.

Summary

An insurance policy is a contract like any other and should be given the appropriate attention. Insureds must be especially diligent to provide all material facts to the insurer. Operators should read all of their insurance contracts in their entirety.

The Parts of an Insurance Policy Other Than a Liability-insurance Policy (21)

Insurance policies may differ from one another according to the type of coverage or to the province in which they are purchased, but most insurance policies are made up of several distinct parts: the declarations, the insuring agreement, statutory conditions (in Quebec, general conditions), policy conditions and a signature clause. The parts of a liability-insurance policy will be presented separately.

The Declarations

This page identifies the parties to the contract (the insured and the insurer); the commencement and expiry dates of the policy; the premium; and the amount of coverage provided; and includes a description of the business that is the object of the coverage.

The Insuring Agreement (the Coverage)

The insuring agreement is the heart of the insurance contract. It states the subject of the insurance and the property covered, the perils insured, the exclusions, and the conditions under which the insured may receive the proceeds of the insurance.

Statutory Conditions (in Quebec, General Conditions)

Statutory conditions outline the rights and responsibilities of the insured and the insurer under the insurance policy. These conditions are required by law to be part of every insurance policy applying to certain types of coverage such as automobile, accident and sickness, and fire insurance. An example of a statutory condition is the obligation of the insurer to pay for a claim within 60 days of receiving the proof of loss from the insured.

Policy Conditions (also Called General Conditions)

Policy conditions are a variety of provisions and clauses that govern the actions of the insurer and the insured under the insurance policy. An example of a policy condition is that all claims must be paid in Canadian currency.

Signature Clause

The insurance policy should be signed by the insurer or by a duly authorized representative. Many policies warn that the declaration page is not binding if the policy is not countersigned by an authorized representative.

The Parts of a Liability-insurance Policy (22)

Although very similar to non-liability-type policies, liability-insurance policies have a few differences, mainly the addition of sections on definitions and exclusions, and the absence of a statutory-conditions section. The liability-insurance policy generally comprises six sections: the declarations, definitions, the insuring agreement, exclusions, conditions and endorsements. The definitions section provides meaning to certain terms used throughout the policy, while the section on exclusions defines the circumstances and terms that limit or exclude coverage. The absence of statutory conditions means not that the conditions are not legal but rather that the government has not legislated the fact that a certain number of conditions have to be part of the policy. In fact, the conditions section in a liability-insurance policy contains numerous conditions with which the insured must comply in order to be covered in the event of a claim. This can be legally enforced via contract law. These conditions will be discussed further in the section on liability insurance.

Endorsements

An endorsement is a document that is used to make changes to an insurance policy. It overrules any wording in the policy. (23) Endorsements are used to restrict or extend the insurance policy's basic coverage and can also be used to make a variety of changes such as address and name changes. They are separate documents that are attached to an insurance policy. Adventure operators should be careful to read and understand all endorsements, as restrictions are commonly put on existing coverage.

Cancelling an Insurance Contract (24)

Insureds can request the cancellation of an insurance policy at any time, and the insurer is then required to refund the excess premium. When an insured asks that a contract be cancelled before its expiry date, the refund will be calculated on a short-rate basis. This means that the insurer will reimburse less than the proportionate part of the premium that is not earned. The portion that is not reimbursed is used to cover the administrative expenses incurred because of the early cancellation. It can also be viewed as a sort of penalty for cancelling the policy before the expiry date.

An insurer can cancel an insurance contract as long as the insured is given an appropriate period of notice and advised by registered mail or personal delivery. The period of notice varies and is usually stipulated in the contract. When an insurer cancels a policy, the refund will be calculated on a pro rata basis. This means that the totality of the unearned premium will be returned, without any penalty to the insured. Policies are most often cancelled for reasons of non-payment, but they can also be cancelled in cases where the insurer discovers material facts that change the nature of the risk or because of claim-related issues.

Summary

Insurance policies are devised in various sections that fulfill different roles. It is important for the insured to read the insurance policy (contract) and to be familiar with all the various conditions and exclusions. Most property and casualty insurance contracts in Canada and the United States are very similar in their purpose, wording, coverage and exclusions. In Canada, the provincial governments have legislated the content and coverage of automobile-insurance policies. This means that two policies purchased from different insurers in the same province will have exactly the same wording and coverage.

Purchasing Insurance

Because of the nature of the activities involved, the options available in the insurance marketplace for adventure operations are much more limited than they are for more "mainstream" types of business activity such as retail businesses. An operator may therefore spend a significant amount of time and energy searching for affordable insurance options. This section will look at how insurers evaluate and rate insurance portfolios and how operators should prepare in order to facilitate their applications for insurance.

The Intermediary's Role

Most if not all adventure operators will purchase their insurance through an insurance broker. In order to evaluate the needs of the insured, the broker will ask the operator a number of questions and will most likely also ask that one or more insurance-application questionnaires be completed. The broker will then submit the insurance applications to one or more insurers in order to obtain different quotes for the insured, which should contain details on coverage, conditions and, of course, the premium.

Evaluation and Rating of an Insurance Portfolio by an Insurer

The object of a particular business' insurance application is referred to by the insurer as a *risk*. (25) Here the word "risk" is used in a specific context and does not mean the chance of loss. For example, when a backcountry-skiing operator submits an application to obtain insurance for his or her lodge, the lodge itself is referred to by the insurer as a risk. The whole company will also be viewed as a risk and classified as a good risk, a bad risk or somewhere in between. It is the job of the underwriter (employed by the insurer) to evaluate the risk (to accept the risk, reject it, or accept it under certain conditions) and to assign it an appropriate premium. This is called *the underwriting process*.

Before discussing the underwriting process, the insurance terms *peril* and *hazard* should be explained. A *peril* is an event that may cause a loss to occur. Insurance is purchased to obtain protection from perils. (26) Examples of perils are fire, wind, theft and, in the case of liability insurance, negligence. A *hazard* is a condition that may cause a peril to occur. Examples of hazards are a poorly maintained building, a wood stove used to dry wet clothes, and even untrained employees. These hazards could cause a peril to happen. For example, untrained employees are a hazard since they are more likely to make mistakes than trained employees, thus causing the peril of negligence to occur.

The Underwriting Process

When evaluating the insurance application, the underwriter must decide whether to accept the risk and, if so, at what premium and under what terms. In order to do this, the underwriter will assess the risk based on the following factors: the moral hazard, the physical hazard, and factors pertaining to the type of risk. (27)

❖ The moral hazard

The moral hazard refers to the likelihood of loss caused by possible deficiencies in the personal character of the insured (the business owner/operator). Examples are the insured's claims history, financial situation and past behaviour.

❖ The physical hazard

The physical hazard refers to the construction, situation, occupancy, condition and exposure of the premises to be insured. Exposure refers to the possibility of loss arising from other tenants or businesses close by. For example, if an operator wants insurance for the canoes that he has stored in a rented space, the underwriter will evaluate the risk and establish the rate based on such things as the construction of the building, the proximity to a fire hall, and the other tenants. If there is a fireworks manufacturer in the building, this will affect the premium of the insured because of the exposure from this other tenant.

❖ Factors pertaining to the type of risk

Any information that will help the underwriter assess the risk is a factor pertaining to the type of risk. This can be statistical information, loss probabilities or social trends. This type of information is especially useful to assess liability-insurance applications where the information relating to the moral and physical sides of the risk is insufficient or irrelevant.

Ratemaking

To establish the appropriate premium for an insurance contract, the underwriter will use predetermined rates that are established by actuaries — statistical specialists who analyse past claim experience and calculate future claim probabilities. The rate is the price for a unit of insurance, while the premium is the rate multiplied by the amount of insurance purchased or, in the case of liability insurance, the rate multiplied by the unit used to establish the premium. (28) For example: The liability-insurance rate for a canoe-tripping operator might be $3.00 per client per day. This rate is then multiplied by the number of client-days (200 clients per day for three days = 600 client-days) to obtain a premium of $1,800.00.

How to Purchase Insurance

Adventure operators should treat the purchase of insurance much like getting a bank loan. The better prepared the operator, the easier it will be to obtain good quotes and a variety of different options. Although all of the different brokers and insurers have their own insurance-application questionnaires, the operator should at least prepare, if only for him- or herself, a basic document outlining the insurance needs of the business. This document will serve as the master and enable the operator to compare the quotes obtained and see if they meet or exceed the insurance needs of the business and if so at what cost. Without advocating the "shop till you drop" approach, it is suggested that operators obtain at least three different quotes from different brokers, as this will provide a good spread of options and prices. The questionnaires and the documentation required to complete the insurance application vary greatly from one broker to another and also from one type of insurance to another (for example, liability versus property insurance). It is important that any insurance matters be dealt with in writing, as this will prevent any potential ambiguities. Remember that insurance is unfortunately only tried and tested when a claim arises, which is usually not a good time to discover that something is missing.

How Much Insurance Should Be Purchased?

This question is not easily answered because businesses vary greatly in their needs, but the golden rule is "You should buy insurance based more on what you can't afford to lose than on what you can afford to pay." In other words, you should buy insurance based on your needs instead of on the amount of money you are willing to devote to insurance.

Which Types of Insurance Should Be Purchased?

Anything can be insured for a price — meaning that anything that needs to be insured can be insured. This section discusses the main types of insurance needed by adventure operators: liability insurance, property insurance, business-interruption insurance, automobile insurance and other types of insurance.

Liability Insurance

For the majority of operators, liability insurance is the most important insurance coverage purchased. It is often the most expensive and, for many, the hardest to find. Without liability insurance, many adventures businesses would not be able to operate. The primary function of liability insurance is to protect operators against liability (lawsuits) arising from the conduct of their businesses. For many, liability insurance means primarily protection against lawsuits from clients who may be injured or killed while under the operator's care.

The Commercial General Liability Insurance Policy (CGL)

The CGL is the most widely used liability-insurance policy in Canada, and it is this policy that is likely to provide coverage to most adventure operators. Although some differences exist, most insurance companies use the version of the CGL that was written by the Insurance Bureau of Canada in 1986. (29) A few insurers still use an older version called the Comprehensive General Liability Insurance Policy.

Coverage under the CGL

The CGL provides coverage for four different types of liability exposure: (30)
   ❖ Bodily-injury and property-damage liability

✧ personal-injury liability
✧ medical payments
✧ tenants' legal liability

Bodily-injury and Property-damage Liability

Under a liability-insurance policy, the insurer will pay the sums that the insured becomes legally obligated to pay as compensatory damages because of bodily injury or property damage to which this insurance applies. The bodily injury or property damage must be caused by an accident or occurrence; the accident or occurrence or the date of claim must occur during the policy period; and the accident or occurrence must take place in the coverage territory. (31)

Legally Obligated

There must be a legal obligation to pay. This prevents the insured from making gratuitous or sympathy payments. For example, a sea-kayaking operator cannot ask his insurance company to pay for a client's boat that was lost in a storm because the operator feels bad about the situation. The insurer will pay only if there is a legal obligation to do so; the client will therefore have to successfully sue the operator for compensation.

Compensatory Damages

The liability-insurance contract only covers compensation for direct damages and does not cover punitive damages or any other sums imposed on the insured as a punishment. Punitive damages are awarded by the courts and are more frequent in the United States.

Bodily Injury and Property Damage

Bodily injury includes physical injuries, sickness, death and psychological injury. (32)

Accident or Occurrence

Most liability-insurance policies sold cover damages on an *occurrence basis* rather than on an *accident basis*. *Occurrence* is defined as an accident involving continuous or repeated exposure to substantially the same general, harmful conditions. The term *accident* is more restrictive and implies suddenness and discreteness. (33) This distinction is important, and adventure operators should make sure that their policies cover occurrences in addition to simply accidents. For example: since hypothermia is caused by continuous exposure rather than being a sudden event, it would not be covered by a policy that provides coverage on an accident-only basis.

Policy Period (Occurrence Policy versus Claims-made Policy)

The *occurrence* policy and the *claims-made* policy differ regarding when coverage is triggered (i.e. when a claim would be covered). The occurrence policy is the most widely used, whereas the claims-made policy is a newer concept that was initiated at the height of the mid-'80s liability-insurance crisis. (34) The difference in coverage between these two types of policies can have a severe impact on an adventure operator. The claims-made policy usually surfaces when the liability-insurance market is in crisis.

❖ *The occurrence policy*

Here an accident (bodily injury or property damage) will be covered if it occurs while the insurance policy is in force. This is the type of liability-insurance policy that is familiar to most insureds. For example, if an operator purchases an occurrence policy covering the period of January 1, 2000, to December 31, 2000, and an accident occurs on June 1, 2000 (during the policy period), the operator is automatically covered even if the claim is not received until April 1, 2001. In summary, an operator is covered by an occurrence policy as long as the accident happens during the policy period.

❖ *The claims-made policy*

Under a claims-made policy, an accident (bodily injury or property damage) will be covered if the claim (not the accident) is made during the policy period. It does not matter whether there was an insurance policy in force at the time of the accident as long as there was a policy in force at the time of the claim. For example: An operator has purchased a claims-made policy covering the period of January 1, 2000, to December 31, 2000, and an accident occurs on June 1, 2000. The operator receives the claim on March 1, 2001. Contrary to the previous example, the operator is not automatically covered. In fact, the operator will only be covered if there is a valid claims-made policy at the time of the claim (March 2, 2001). In summary, an operator is covered by a claims-made policy as long as the claim is made during the policy period.

The Impact on the Operator and His or Her Insurance-buying Strategy

If an operator purchases occurrence liability-insurance policies year after year, there is not much to be worried about since it does not matter when the claim is made as long as the occurrence policy was in force at the time of the accident. On the other hand, if the operator is insured by a claims-made liability-insurance policy, he or she must keep purchasing a claims-made policy as long as there is the possibility of a claim. This means that if an operator offers adventure activities for only one season, he or she must continue to buy a claims-made insurance policy until the threat of a lawsuit is gone. Other difficult situations can develop, such as when an operator switches insurance companies and goes from an occurrence policy to a claims-made policy. It is likely that the new insurer will be unwilling to cover claims for past years of operation and will put restrictions on the back period it is willing to cover. In summary, claims-made policies should be avoided if possible; in cases where this is not an option, operators should thoroughly discuss the implications with an insurance expert.

Coverage Territory

Most liability-insurance policies restrict coverage to a certain geographical area, although some are now sold with worldwide coverage. For example, the standard CGL covers operations in Canada and in the United States and its territories and possessions. (35) Adventure operators should make sure that their liability insurance covers them in the countries in which they operate, especially if they run programs outside Canada and the United States.

Personal-injury Liability

The CGL also provides coverage for a different type of personal injury, namely injury to the character, reputation and position of a third party caused by libel or slander. The intent is to cover offenses arising from the conduct of the insured's business. (36) Intentional damages are excluded.

Medical Payments

This section provides coverage for medical expenses incurred by a third party, without the need to prove negligence or establish any legal obligation on the part of the insured. This coverage is seen as a goodwill gesture that might prevent further legal action. (37)

Tenants' Legal Liability

Under the CGL, the insured can be covered for damages to the premises he or she is renting or occupying (without owning). (38) This coverage is not always automatic; if it has not been offered, it must be specifically requested by the insured. For example, an operator renting office or storage space must purchase tenants' legal-liability insurance to be covered for potential damages caused by the operator to the rented premises.

Exclusions

Each of the above insuring agreements has its own series of exclusions, and each CGL has a series of general exclusions that are common to all coverages. Although the exclusions are part of the wording of the basic policy, they can be modified or removed using endorsements. Some of these exclusions may be more relevant to some operators than others. The following are the main exclusions (among many) common to most CGL policies:

❖ *Intentional injury or damage*

Injuries or damage that are willful or reckless in nature are excluded.

❖ *Contractual liability*

The liability arising from contracts or any breach of contract is generally excluded, except for those contracts covered under the definition of insured contracts. This exclusion does not mean that all contracts are excluded. For example, if it is proved that liability would have been imposed by law even in the absence of the contract, the contract is not excluded. Contracts can be covered with the permission of the insurer — usually with a surcharge, if applicable.

✧ **Workers' compensation and employees**
Liability insurance does not apply to bodily injury to an employee of the insured during the course of his or her employment except if assumed under an insured contract. For example, an insurer agrees to cover an operator who assumes, by contract, responsibility regarding workers' compensation for his or her employees working in a foreign country. Liability insurance does not apply to any obligation for which the insured may be held liable under workers' compensation law. (39)

✧ **Automobile, watercraft and aircraft**
The liability-insurance policy does not apply to bodily injury or property damage arising out of the ownership, maintenance, use or operation, loading and unloading of any automobile, watercraft, motorized snow vehicle, or aircraft. Liability coverage arising out of the use of these vehicles is covered under separate insurance policies. For example, the liability arising out of the use of an automobile is covered by an automobile policy. (40)

✧ **Care custody and control**
Property that is owned, rented or occupied by the insured, or property for which the insured has care custody and control, is not covered under the liability-insurance policy. These property items can be covered by other insurance contracts. The tenants' legal-liability coverage under the CGL (*see above*), if included, will compensate for this exclusion as it relates to rented premises.

✧ **Product and performance**
The intent of the liability-insurance policy is to cover any bodily injury or property damage that might be caused to another by the operator's product and services. The policy is not intended to cover poor service or bad products. For example, the insurer will not consider a claim where the insured was forced to reimburse dissatisfied clients. (41)

✧ **Pollution**
This exclusion is very broad and usually excludes any type of pollution or environmental damage.

✧ **Other exclusions**
The CGL and all the other liability-insurance policies contain several additional exclusions. It is strongly suggested that every operator be familiar with all of them. Many of the exclusions can be eliminated through endorsements or through the purchase of complementary insurance policies.

Who Can Be an Insured

The CGL will cover not only the person(s) or business named as the insured in the declarations but also the following: in the case of an individual, his or her spouse; in the case of a partnership or joint venture, the partnership and joint venture members and their spouses; in the case of an organization other than a partnership or joint venture, the organization itself and its executive officers, directors and stockholders.

Also covered are the employees of the named insured within the scope of their employment (bodily injury to the employees themselves is excluded). (42) Besides the named insured, it is possible to add additional insureds such as governments, land owners, or any other party wanting to be covered by the operator's policy.

Supplementary Payments

In addition to paying for compensatory damages arising from claims against the insured, the insurer will also pay for certain types of expenses such as the fees associated with the legal defense of the insured. These defense fees also include other fees associated with a claim (evaluators, adjusters, experts and investigators) and are above and beyond the stipulated insurance limit. In other words, payment of these fees will not reduce the amount available for compensatory damages.

Limits of Insurance

The declarations page of the CGL policy specifies the limits for the various coverages provided under the policy. These limits are the maximum amounts the insurer will pay regardless of the number of insureds or of claims made and generally comprise the following: (43)

- ❖ The **aggregate limit** is the maximum total amount payable by the policy in the policy period (usually one year), regardless of the number of claims or lawsuits.
- ❖ The **occurrence limit** is the maximum payable for any one occurrence for any type or combination of damage (bodily injury, property damage, personal injury, tenants' legal liability or medical payments).
- ❖ The **tenants' legal-liability limit** is the maximum amount payable because of property damage to any one premises rented by an insured.
- ❖ The **personal-injury limit** is the maximum amount payable for personal injury sustained by any one person or organization.
- ❖ The **medical-expense limit** is the maximum medical-expense amount payable per person and per accident.
- ❖ Many policies have a **decreasing limit**, meaning that after a claim has been paid the amount of insurance available for the next claim is decreased by the amount of that payment (*see Figure 13–3 for an example*).

Conditions

Every liability-insurance policy includes a certain number of conditions that are an integral part of the policy. These conditions outline the rights and duties of both the insurer and the insured.

Figure 13–3 ❖ *Example of Liability-insurance Limits*

Commercial General Liability Insurance Policy

Insurer: The Safe Insurance Company   **Policy No.:** 564–876
Insured: The Adventure Company
Policy Period: January 1, 2000, to December 31, 2000

Limits of Insurance

Each occurrence limit	$2,000,000	Aggregate limit	$2,000,000
Personal-injury limit	$2,000,000	Tenants' legal-liability limit	$100,000
Medical-expense limit	$1,000/10,000 (any one person/any one accident)		

The insured negligently causes a fire in the premises he rents to store his equipment. Three of the insured's clients are also injured in the fire. They are transported to the hospital.

The following damages and expenses are incurred:

Damage to the rented premises	$ 110,000
Bodily injury to clients	750,000
Ambulance transportation	150
Total	**$ 860,150**

The policy will pay:

Tenants' legal liability (max. payable)	$ 100,000
Bodily injury	750,000
Medical payments	150
Total	**$ 850,150**

Total amount of insurance available for the remainder of the policy period:

(aggregate limit: $2,000,000) – (losses: $850,150)

= (**insurance available**: $1,149,850)

Some of the conditions are trivial, while others are quite important. For example, one of the conditions outlines the duties of the insured in the case of a claim, while another outlines the right of the insurer to examine the insured's books and records. It goes without saying that operators should be familiar with all of the conditions of their liability-insurance policies.

The Premium

The insurer will generally calculate the liability-insurance premium based on estimates of sales, number of clients, square footage and other information. The premium is generally adjustable, meaning that at the end of the year the insurer can ask the insured to provide data on the total number of clients or total sales for the year. This data will be compared to the estimates, and a premium adjustment will be made, resulting in the insured receiving a refund or having to pay a surcharge. The original liability-insurance policy is usually issued with a minimum retained premium — the minimum premium paid by the insured regardless of total sales or total number of clients for the year. For example: A liability-insurance policy is issued with a premium of $2,000 based on projections of 50 clients for the year. The policy has a minimum retained premium of $1,500 and an adjustment rate of $40 per client. At the end of the year, the operator declares that she had only 25 clients during the year. The policy will be adjusted by 25 clients at $40 per client, which equals $1,000. According to the calculations, the operator would be eligible for a $1,000 refund ($2,000 original premium – $1,000 adjusted premium). But because the minimum retained premium is $1,500, the client will only receive a $500 refund. In the event of the policy being cancelled, the minimum retained premium will also apply. The insurer will therefore always keep a minimum of $1,500 regardless of how long the policy is in force.

The Liability-insurance Application

The adventure operator may be required to complete a questionnaire and to provide certain documents in order to obtain a quote and/or coverage. Typically, questions will cover (but not be limited to) the following: a description of the company and its operations and activities; information regarding the owner's experience and the employees' certification and qualifications; safety measures, safety equipment and client-guide ratios; and a description of previous claims. The operator may also be asked to submit a copy of the liability-release document (waiver) used, the emergency-response plan, the risk-management plan, the pre-trip safety talk and the client information package. The information and documentation required may vary considerably from one insurer to another.

Things to Watch out For

Coverage of Participants

Some liability-insurance policies still define their coverage as third-party liability. This can cause problems, as the clients of an adventure operator are not considered third-party but rather are part of the supplier-client contract. Certain adventure operators are also unknowingly being sold liability-insurance policies that exclude bodily injuries to participants. (44) All operators should require written confirmation that bodily injury and property damage to participants are covered under the liability-insurance policy.

Deductibles

Most liability-insurance policies have a deductible (an amount of the loss which the insured must pay), (45) but in some cases the deductible is tied to the use of the liability waiver. For example: Some policies state that if a client sues the operator the deductible will be in the amount of $1,000 only if the operator can provide a copy of the liability waiver signed by the client (plaintiff). Without a copy of the liability waiver, the deductible becomes $25,000. This is an incentive to persuade operators to always use liability waivers.

Endorsements

Many endorsements are available to extend the basic coverage, or to remove exclusions from the basic CGL policy. Some of these endorsements are automatically added to a CGL free of charge; these additions are the responsibility of the insurance broker. On the other hand, endorsements are also used to reduce coverage, usually following legal trends. For example, some endorsements exclude certain types of activities such as mountain biking while others exclude situations that might be hard to fight in court, such as damages caused by the selling, offering or serving of alcoholic beverages.

Other Types of Liability-insurance Policies

The coverage provided by a CGL may not be sufficient to satisfy every operator's liability-insurance needs. Many other types of liability-insurance policy are available on the insurance marketplace. Some of these policies provide coverage for specific risks — for example, directors' and officers' liability insurance — while others provide additional liability insurance for adventure operators who have to manage potential catastrophic losses — for example, excess-liability insurance and umbrella insurance.

The Excess-liability Insurance Policy

As the name implies, this type of liability insurance provides insurance in excess of an existing liability policy. For example: If an operator has a CGL policy with a $2-million-dollar limit and his existing insurer is not prepared to offer a higher limit, the operator can purchase an excess-liability policy from a different insurer — in the additional amount of $2 million, for instance. This will provide the operator with a total liability-coverage limit of $4 million. Generally, the conditions and coverage of the excess policy are exactly the same as those of the primary CGL policy. One of the advantages is that the premium charged for the additional $2 million of excess insurance may be lower than that for the first $2 million. (46)

The Umbrella Insurance Policy

The umbrella policy is similar to the excess-liability policy in the sense that it provides additional liability insurance. But unlike the excess policy, the umbrella policy provides broader coverage than the primary CGL policy. The wording and coverage vary widely from one umbrella policy to another, so every policy should be analysed carefully. If the umbrella policy does not provide broader coverage than the primary CGL, it is nothing more than an excess-liability policy. The reason it is called an umbrella policy is that it provides additional liability insurance over and above all of the liability coverage provided by all of the insured's insurance policies. For example, the umbrella policy can provide additional liability coverage to the CGL policy, the automobile insurance policy, the watercraft insurance policy or any other policy that offers liability coverage. The deductible under an umbrella policy is generally quite substantial; $10,000 is a common amount. (47)

The Directors' and Officers' Liability-insurance Policy

Individuals acting as directors and officers of organizations can be held personally responsible for the decisions they make on behalf of their organization, whether this organization is big or small, non-profit or for profit. They can be held liable for a variety of reasons (lack of growth, financial problems, improper expenditures and many other reasons). Directors' and officers' liability insurance provides protection to directors and officers against liability arising out of wrongful acts, negligence and errors and omissions. One of the major exclusions of this type of policy is that bodily injuries and property damage are not covered. This exclusion can have a significant impact on outdoor/adventure organizations where bodily injuries are a main concern. The organization must purchase a CGL to cover bodily injury and property damage to participants and third parties. (48)

Summary

Liability insurance is one of the main risk-management tools of adventure operators, and the commercial general liability (CGL) insurance policy is the most commonly used liability-insurance policy. Operators should make sure that all their business operations and their participants are covered by their CGL policy. Operators should also be familiar with the CGL's exclusions and endorsements. Many of the risks not covered by the CGL can be covered by other types of liability-insurance policies.

Property Insurance

For many operators, insuring their property is as important, if not more important, than protecting themselves against liability claims. Property insurance is necessary in order to protect insureds against the financial risks associated with the loss of assets such as buildings, equipment, merchandise and supplies. Property insurance basically covers all physical assets except moving vehicles such as automobiles, aircraft, watercraft and snowcraft, which are covered by specific contracts. There are dozens of different policies available on the marketplace which provide coverage for these assets. Some policies only cover specific assets, while others provide coverage for a variety of assets under one policy. Most property-insurance policies have a number of similar features and conditions in common.

All-risk and Named-peril Policies

Property-insurance policies are usually classified according to the perils they insure into two general types: *named-peril policies* and *all-risk policies*.

Named-peril policies only provide coverage for the perils mentioned; if the peril is not mentioned, it is not covered. The named perils usually covered are fire and lightning; explosion; impact by vehicles (land or air crafts); riot; vandalism; smoke; leakage from fire-protection equipment; windstorm; and hail. The named-peril policy also contains a number of exclusions. (49)

The all-risk policy, on the other hand, covers all perils except the ones that are excluded; if the peril is not excluded, it is covered. All-risk policies provide a much broader coverage than do named-peril policies. Common names for the all-risk policies are Commercial Building Form (CBF) and Commercial Property Floater Form (CPF). (50) The all-risk policy contains numerous exclusions that should be familiar to every insured.

Actual Cash Value and Replacement Cost

Following a loss, the insurer will indemnify the insured for the damaged property based on the *actual cash value* of the property or on the *replacement cost* of the property. Actual cash value refers to the actual value of the property at the date of loss, taking into account physical depreciation and wear and tear, and also the actual value of the property on the market. For example: A raft purchased 10 years ago for $3500 might have an actual cash value of $500. The insured would have to make up for the difference in order to purchase a new raft. In order to avoid this, replacement-cost insurance is available. Replacement-cost insurance pays for the full cost of replacement or repair, without any deduction for depreciation. In the above example, the insurer would pay for a new raft of the same type and quality regardless of the cost. One of the main conditions of replacement-cost insurance is that the item must be replaced; if not, the insurer will indemnify based on actual cash value. Replacement-cost insurance does not cost anything itself, but the amount of insurance carried must reflect the replacement cost of the property insured. For example: If an operator knows that her 20-year-old lodge would cost $200,000 to rebuild today, she would have to buy $200,000 of insurance to benefit from the replacement-cost endorsement. If the operator purchases only $100,000 worth of insurance because that is what the lodge is worth today, she will only be indemnified based on the actual cash value of the lodge. Although there is no charge for the actual replacement-cost coverage, the increased insurance limit will of course result in a higher premium.

The Coinsurance Clause

Most people are not familiar with this clause or do not understand it; yet the majority of property-insurance contracts on the market contain a *coinsurance clause* of 80%, 90% or 100%. Furthermore, insureds are often penalized by the coinsurance clause during a claim settlement. The coinsurance clause requires that the amount of insurance on a certain type of property represent at least 80%, 90% or 100% of the actual value of that property. If the insured does not abide by the percentage, he or she will have to share part of the loss and thus become coinsurer. For example: An operator owns canoe and camping equipment that is valued at a replacement cost of $100,000. The operator decides to only purchase $40,000 of insurance, thinking that this is enough coverage and that the premium is within his budget. The policy contains a coinsurance clause of 80%. A small fire in the warehouse destroys $10,000 worth of the equipment. This is how the coinsurance will be applied by the insurer:

Value of equipment		$100,000
Coinsurance 80%	(80% of $100,000)	80,000
Insurance purchased		40,000
Loss		10,000

The $40,000 of insurance purchased is equivalent to 50% of the minimum needed according to the coinsurance clause ($40,000 ÷ $80,000). Since the insured purchased only 50% of the required amount, the insurer will pay only 50% of the loss, or $5,000. If the insured had purchased insurance of $60,000, which represents 75% of the required amount ($60,000 ÷ $80,000), the insurer would have paid 75% of the loss, or $7,500. If the insured had purchased at least $80,000 of insurance, he would not have been penalized. (51)

It is important that operators understand the coinsurance clause and carefully evaluate the value of their property every year to ensure that the clause is respected. One possible alternative for those not wanting to insure all of their property or equipment is to purchase an insurance policy that will only cover the items listed in that policy. This type of policy would enable a canoe-tripping operator to only insure the canoes listed on the policy. Of course, the amount of insurance on these canoes would need to satisfy the coinsurance clause of that particular contract.

Exclusions

Because of the variety of property-insurance contracts, it is impossible to cover all possible exclusions except to say that many of them can be removed through the use of endorsements. For example, earthquakes are excluded from almost any property-insurance contract but can be added through an endorsement. Again, it is imperative that all operators familiarize themselves with their property-insurance contracts. Also, there is a popular belief that all acts of God are excluded from insurance contracts. This is not necessarily true, since many natural events such as wind, hail and lightning are covered.

Different Types of Property Insurance

There are many other types of property-insurance policies serving particular purposes. Some policies specifically cover computers and electronic data processing, valuable papers and records, office equipment and more. Business owners should work with their brokers to make sure that all important assets are covered by the appropriate insurance contract.

Business-interruption Insurance

Business-interruption insurance is not as well known or as popular as other forms of insurance. Although it is not property insurance per se, business-interruption insurance is part of the property-insurance sector. For many adventure operators, especially those who own and depend on their accommodation revenues, business-interruption insurance could mean the difference between disaster and survival. The purpose of this insurance is to replace business income until business returns to normal. If a backcountry-skiing lodge burns down in late November, it is unlikely that the operator would be able to rebuild until the spring; he or she would therefore lose all the revenues of the busy winter season. Business-interruption policies provide coverage on a named-peril or an all-risk basis just as do property-insurance policies. There are three types of policies available: *profits*, *gross-earnings* and *extra-expense* policies. *Profits* and *gross-earnings* policies both offer income-restoration coverage, the main difference between the two being the period of indemnity. The profits policy will replace revenues until earnings are back at the same level as prior to the loss, whereas the gross-earnings policy will replace revenues only until the business is rebuilt and ready to operate. Both these policies have a maximum indemnity period of 12 months after the date of loss. The *extra-expense* policy will cover the extra expenses incurred by the business in order to stay in operation. For example, this type of policy could cover the extra expenses involved in sending clients to a hotel while the lodge is repaired. (52)

Automobile Insurance

Automobile liability insurance for private and commercial vehicles is mandatory throughout Canada. Each provincial and territorial government sets its own minimum amount of liability coverage. Coverage for damages to the vehicle itself is available on a voluntary basis. (53) All of the standard automobile-insurance policies in Canada have been legislated by the provincial and territorial governments; the wording of two different policies from the same province should therefore be identical. The standard automobile policy is similar across all the provinces and territories, except in Quebec. In Manitoba, Quebec (liability insurance only), Saskatchewan and British Columbia, automobile insurance is sold by the provincial government. Except in Quebec, automobile insurance is actually a combination of three different coverages:

  ✤ third-party-liability coverage for liability arising from bodily injuries or death and for liability arising from property damage
  ✤ accident and disability coverage for the insured, including coverage for uninsured motorists who are the cause of the accident
  ✤ damage to the insured's vehicle (collision, comprehensive, specified perils).

Additional coverages are available through endorsements. Because of its standardization, automobile insurance is usually not a complicated purchase. The problems, if any, are encountered in the claim process. For example, it is sometimes discovered that the real use of the vehicle (commercial use) was different from the use indicated when the premium was established (pleasure use).

Other Types of Insurance

Since most motorized transportation vehicles are excluded from regular property- and liability-insurance policies, separate insurance contracts must be purchased to cover these vehicles. Operators using boats (other than canoes and kayaks) in their operations must obtain marine insurance to cover both the boats and any liability arising from the use of the boats. Operators using aircraft must obtain aviation insurance. If the operator is contracting out this type of service, proof of insurance should be obtained from the contractor. Exposure can still exist even when one does not own one of these vehicles. (54) Other vehicles such as snowmobiles and motorcycles are also subject to separate insurance policies.

Rescue Insurance

This is a very specialized market where operators can obtain insurance to cover the costs of rescues and evacuations. Coverage can be provided in two different ways: the operator can purchase a blanket rescue-insurance policy that will cover all rescues and evacuations over a certain period, or the clients themselves can purchase individual rescue insurance for a particular trip.

The Claim Process

Insurance is only a promise, until it is tested when the insured suffers a loss. Insurance then becomes a tangible product. This section is not intended to teach claim adjustment but rather to explain the major steps in the claim process, the roles of the different players, and some of the terminology involved.

The Players in a Claim

The *insurance broker* should be the first person contacted in the event of a claim and should also be a key player in the claim process. He or she will report the claim to the insurer and should work on behalf of the insured. The broker can have some influence in the decision-making process, but his or her real power is somewhat limited. The *adjuster* is the person who will handle the claim on behalf of the insurer. Adjusters can be employees of the insurer, or they can be independent adjusters. Adjusters investigate the claim, obtain all the necessary facts, determine if there is coverage, establish the amount of the loss and recommend the amount of payment if the loss is covered by the insurance contract. Depending on the type and size of the claim, a variety of experts and evaluators will be involved in determining coverage, and/or the value of the loss. *Public adjusters* are independent adjusters who can be hired by the insured to represent the insured's interest during a claim. These adjusters are paid by the insured, usually based on a percentage of the claim. (55)

Elements of a Claim

Once the claim is ready to be settled, the insurer will have the insured sign a document called a *proof of loss*. This document contains various details including the final amount of the claim and to whom it should be paid. When the insured signs the proof-of-loss document, the insurer is released from further obligations relating to the loss and all salvageable items are transferred to the insurer. (56) If during the investigation the insurer is suspicious about the claim, it will have the insured sign a document called a *non-waiver agreement* indicating that the insurer will continue its investigation of the claim but that it retains the right to deny coverage. The requirement that a non-waiver agreement be signed is a clear indication that something might be wrong with the claim and that the insured might not be indemnified for the loss. (57) All contracts of indemnity (insurance) contain a *subrogation clause*. Subrogation gives the insurer the right to recover from the responsible party the sums that have be paid to the insured. (58) For example, if the neighbouring tenant in the building where the operator stores her equipment causes a fire that damages the operator's equipment, the operator's insurer will indemnify the operator and then by subrogation will recover the sums paid from the tenant who was responsible for the fire.

The Onus of Proof

In most insurance claims (other than liability), it is the responsibility of the insured to prove that he or she did suffer the damages reported and that the cause of the loss is insured under the insurance policy. Once the insured has established coverage and the amount of the loss, it is the obligation of the insurer to pay the claim or deny coverage. (59) For example, an operator must prove that he did own the canoes that he claims were stolen and he must prove their value as well as the cause of the loss. Only reasonable proof needs to be provided.

Liability-insurance Claims

The conditions section of the liability-insurance policy contains instructions on the insured's duties in case of an accident, occurrence, claim or suit. It states that the insured should inform the insurer (via the broker) as soon as he or she is made aware of a claim or any circumstances that might produce a claim. This means that operators should advise their insurance brokers of any incident that might produce a claim and should not wait to receive a lawsuit. This may enable the insurer to start an investigation and minimize the size of the loss. The conditions also state that the insured should cooperate with the insurer and assist in making settlements. An important warning is included stating that if an insured admits responsibility and/or tries to make a settlement by him- or herself, he or she is causing a prejudice to the insurer. Failure to comply with these conditions could result in the insurer not honouring the claim at all, or doing so under a non-waiver agreement.

After a Claim Is Reported

Once a claim or incident has been reported, the insurer will take over the entire defense and direct the defense strategies, using its own lawyers and investigators. If the insured wants his or her own lawyer, he or she will have to pay the costs of that lawyer. The insurer will usually adopt a defense strategy that tries to pay the lowest amount possible. This often means settling a claim out of court at a lesser cost even though it might make the operator look negligent or guilty, rather than risking higher legal costs by fighting a case in court to prove the operator's innocence.

The Guide and Insurance

It is in the best interest of a guide employed as a contractor or employee to inquire about his or her employer's insurance coverage. Most importantly, the guide should know if he or she is covered under the liability-insurance policy of the employer. If so, the guide may want to see the policy in order to assess the extent of the coverage provided. For example: An operator might adhere to the popular strategy of "less insurance is better", which might be contrary to a particular guide's own philosophy. If the guide is not covered under the employer's policy, she might have to provide her own insurance or accept the risk of working without insurance coverage. Guides will also want to look into acquiring insurance to protect their equipment. This can be done through the employer's insurance policy, by purchasing a stand-alone insurance policy or by adding the equipment to an existing homeowner's insurance policy. Equipment used professionally is not covered under personal-insurance contracts unless it is added by endorsement.

Insurance-portfolio Management

The management of the insurance portfolio of a business should consist of more than paying the insurance bill and filing the contracts until the following year. Someone should be assigned to this portfolio and a relationship should be established with the insurance broker. The limits of insurance, the coverage and the conditions should be revised at least once a year. Insurance contracts should be read in their entirety and understood. Whoever handles the insurance portfolio should be quite familiar with the business operations, as this person will have to educate the broker and/or the insurer on the specific nature of the activities and the risks involved.

Insurance Issues and the Adventure Industry

Insurance Cycles

Many operators believed that the mid-1980s liability-insurance crisis would never end and that this was a sign of things to come. Although major changes occurred because of it, the crisis was short-lived and was over within a few years. (60) At the time of this writing, we find ourselves in a relatively soft liability-insurance market, with reasonably affordable premiums, good availability of coverage and a high number of insurance providers. (61) Again, the current situation may be short-lived and should not be taken as an indication of things to come. Insurance is a cyclical industry, and another crisis should be expected. (62)

Insurance and Legal-release Documents (Waivers)

In many parts of Canada, waivers have become very successful in avoiding costly claims settlements for insurers. Insurers know the importance and effectiveness of waivers and take this knowledge into consideration when assessing risks and establishing policy conditions and premiums. For example, many insurers have added a condition to their liability-insurance contracts which ties the policy deductible to the liability-release document. This condition usually states that, in the event of a claim being made by a client for which a waiver was not signed or is not available, the deductible will become much higher ($25,000, for instance). This condition serves as clear incentive for operators to always use waivers. This is the current situation. The future may look very different. The day may come when waivers are not, for many reasons, as effective and successful as they are today. We can only assume that the insurance marketplace might react quite drastically to such a turnaround. Although this is pure speculation, such a change alone could affect the availability of liability insurance.

The Role of Associations in Insurance

Many industry, sports and professional associations play a key role in the management of insurance portfolios for their members. The most significant benefit is the increased purchase power of a group. In theory, this increased purchase power usually translates into lower premiums, better coverage, more negotiating power, and more flexibility in times of crisis. In reality, group-insurance programs are not easy to start or manage and must be large enough to provide insurers with a substantial amount of revenue. Another major benefit of groups and associations is the collection of statistical data that is badly needed in the adventure-tourism industry. Statistics would certainly help the industry in its future attempts to prove its safety record.

Notes to Chapter Thirteen

1. Insurance Institute of Canada; C16 (1997).
2. Ibid.
3. Insurance Institute of Canada; C11 (1997).
4. Insurance Council of Canada, 1998.
5. Ibid.
6. Insurance Institute of Canada; C11 (1997).
   Insurance Council of Canada, 1998.
7. Insurance Institute of Canada; C11 (1997).
   Insurance Council of Canada, 1998.
   Insurance Institute of Canada; C16 (1997).
   Insurance Institute of Canada; C72 (1997).
8. Insurance Institute of Canada; C16 (1997).
9. Ibid.
10. Insurance Council of Canada, 1998.
11. Insurance Council of Canada.
12. Insurance Institute of Canada; C16 (1997).
13. Insurance Institute of Canada; C11 (1997).
14. Insurance Institute of Canada; C16 (1997).
15. Ibid.
16. Hilliker (1996), p. 14.
17. Insurance Institute of Canada; C11 (1997), ch. 9, p. 2.
18. Hilliker (1996), p. 19.
19. Insurance Institute of Canada; C11 (1997), ch. 9, p. 6.
20. Ibid., p. 14.
21. Ibid., ch. 10, p.15.
22. Hilliker (1996), p. 23.
23. Insurance Institute of Canada; C11 (1997), ch. 10, p. 26.
24. Ibid., p. 10.
25. Ibid., ch. 3, p. 13.
26. Ibid., p. 8.
27. Ibid.
28. Ibid., p. 2.
29. Hilliker (1996), p. 114.
30. Insurance Institute of Canada; C13 (1997), ch. 8, p. 5.
31. Ibid., p. 6.
32. Hilliker (1996), p. 134.
33. Insurance Institute of Canada; C13 (1997), ch. 8, p. 7.
34. Hilliker (1996), p. 156.
35. Insurance Institute of Canada; C13 (1997), ch. 8, p. 8.

36. Ibid., p. 16.

37. Ibid.

38. Ibid., p. 18.

39. Hilliker (1996), p.180.

40. Insurance Institute of Canada; C13 (1997), ch. 8, p. 11.

41. Hilliker (1996), p.173.

42. Insurance Institute of Canada; C13 (1997), ch. 8, p. 21.

43. Ibid., p. 22.

44. Huestis (1999)

45. Insurance Institute of Canada; C11 (1997), ch. 10, p. 11.

46. Insurance Institute of Canada; C72 (1996), ch. 8, p. 16.

47. Ibid., p. 17.

48. Insurance Institute of Canada; C13 (1997), ch. 9, p. 19–23.

49. Insurance Institute of Canada; C72 (1996), ch. 6, p. 11–13.

50. Ibid., ch. 7, p. 2.

51. Ibid., ch. 6, p. 6-7.

52. Ibid., ch. 9, p. 6-7.

53. Insurance Council of Canada, 1998.

54. Ibid., ch. 4, p. 23.

55. Insurance Institute of Canada; C11 (1997), ch. 11, p. 3-5.

56. Ibid., p. 8.

57. Ibid., p. 13.

58. Ibid., p. 19.

59. Ibid., p. 16–17.

60. Insurance Institute of Canada; C16 (1997), ch. 5, p. 15.

61. Valade (1997), p. 1.

62. Ibid., p. 5.

Bibliography

Bernstein, Peter L. *Against the Gods: The Remarkable Story of Risk*. John Wiley and Sons Inc., 1996.

Bird, Stephen, and John Zauhar. *Recreation and the Law* (Second Edition). Thompson Canada Ltd., 1997.

Cloutier, K.R. *The Business of Adventure: Developing an Adventure Tourism Business*. Kamloops: Bhudak Consultants Ltd., 1998.

Conn, L., and S. Van Zyl. "Risk Management: Evolution of a Profession". *Canadian Underwriter*, 66, 3 (1999).

Fridman, G.H.L. *The Law of Contract* (Third Edition). Thompson Canada Ltd., 1994.

Hilker, G. *Liability Insurance Law in Canada*. Vancouver: Butterworths Canada Ltd., 1996.

Hill, Charles, and Gareth Jones. *Strategic Management Theory: An Integrated Approach*. Houghton, Mifflin Company, 1998.

Hronek, Bruce, and J.O. Spengler. *Legal Liability in Recreation and Sports*. Sagamore Publishing, 1997.

Huestis, P. (The Huestis Insurance Group, St-John, New Brunswick). Personal conversation. November 26, 1999.

Insurance Council of Canada. "Facts of the General Insurance Industry in Canada". Toronto: 1998

Insurance Institute of Canada. *C11: Principles and Practice of Insurance*. Toronto: 1997.

Insurance Institute of Canada. *C13: Insurance against Liability*. Toronto: 1997.

Insurance Institute of Canada. *C16: The Business of Insurance*. Toronto: 1997.

Insurance Institute of Canada. *C72: Introduction to Risk Management and Commercial Lines Insurance*. Toronto: 1997.

Klar, Lewis N. *Tort Law*. Thompson Canada Ltd., 1991

Linden, Allen. *Canadian Tort Law* (Fifth Edition). Butterworths Canada Ltd., 1993.

MacKay, Wayne, and Lyle Sutherland. *Teachers and the Law: A Practical Guide for Educators*. Emond Montgomery Publications Ltd., 1992.

Smyth, J.E., et al. *The Law and Business Administration in Canada*. Prentice-Hall Canada Ltd., 1991.

Spetz, S.N., and G.S. Spetz. **The Rule of Law: Canadian Business Law** (Second Edition). Copp Clark Ltd., 1995.

Valade. **Legal Liability and Liability Insurance Study and Position Paper of the New Brunswick Outdoor and Adventure Tourism Industry**. Fredericton: Ministry of Economic Development and Tourism, 1997.

Vaughan, Emmett J. **Fundamentals of Risk and Insurance** (Sixth Edition). John Wiley & Sons, 1992.

Wasserman, Natalie, and Dean Phelus. **Risk Management Today**. Risk and Insurance Management Association of the United States and the International City Management Association, 1985.

Willes, John. **Contemporary Canadian Business Law** (Fourth Edition). McGraw-Hill Ryerson Ltd., 1994.

Index

The Authors

Ross Cloutier

Ross Cloutier is a climbing guide who has been involved in mountain guiding and mountain rescue for over 25 years. He was the climbing leader for the 1991 Canadian Everest Expedition and has first ascents in numerous countries. Ross has studied recreation administration and outdoor pursuits and has an MBA in international business.

Ross has been involved in organizing expeditions and guiding journeys to 25 countries. For many years, he owned an adventure business that guided clients to high peaks around the world. He also founded a heli-ski-touring and hiking business in the Cariboo Mountains. Between 1989 and 1992, he was the provincial search and rescue training co-ordinator at the Justice Institute of British Columbia. He developed the Adventure Guide diploma and degree programs now offered at the University College of the Cariboo in Kamloops, British Columbia.

Ross is the author of over 30 publications, the most recent of which is his book *The Business of Adventure: Developing an Adventure Tourism Business*. He presents at numerous symposia and conferences around North America and holds risk-management workshops for government and business interests.

Dan Garvey

Dan Garvey has been professionally involved in experiential education for over 25 years. He is currently a faculty member at the University of New Hampshire, where he specializes in the areas of cross-cultural education and moral development. Before joining the University of New Hampshire, his positions as an administrator and practitioner included vice-president of the American Youth Foundation, St. Louis, Missouri; president and executive director of the Association for Experiential Education (AEE), Boulder, Colorado; and dean of the Semester at Sea program, University of Pittsburgh. Dan was the 1997 recipient of the AEE Kurt Hahn Award.

Dan holds degrees in sociology and in social change and received his Ph.D. from the University of Colorado in social and multicultural studies. He is listed in *Who's Who in American Education* and *Who's Who in World Education*. Dan has authored more than 20 books and articles dealing with the broad topic of experiential education.

Will Leverette

Will Leverette has been an active member of the professional outdoor-education/recreation community for 25 years. He was the staff coordinator and program developer for a therapeutic camping program for juvenile delinquents in North Carolina for eight years. He has been a whitewater river paddler for 35 years and was an instructor trainer with the American Canoe

Association for 12 years. He was a water-safety, advanced-first-aid, CPR and canoeing instructor with the American Red Cross for 10 years.

For the last 11 years, Will has worked as a risk manager and claims consultant to the liability-insurance industry with the Worldwide Outfitter and Guide Association. He now owns his own risk- and crisis-management consulting business, ARMOR: the Affiliation of Risk Managers for Outdoor Recreation. He also coaches the Warren Wilson College Whitewater Paddling Team, which was undefeated on the collegiate circuit for five years.

James Moss

Jim Moss is a risk-management consultant and a U.S. trial attorney who is the author of the *Lawyer's Advisor and Outdoor Recreation Forms* manuals. He consults with service-oriented industries to decrease their chances of being sued. His writing has appeared in numerous publications including *Outside Business* and *The Outdoor Network*. He has made presentations to Colorado attorneys in continuing-education courses and to the Wilderness Medical Society, the Western River Guides Association, the Professional Paddlesports Association, the Boy Scouts of America, the International Conference on Outdoor Recreation, the Wilderness Education Association and federal land-management agencies.

Jim has taught rock climbing and mountaineering and currently works as an outdoor guide for whitewater-rafting companies in Colorado, Utah and Arizona. He is a member of the Adventure Sports Lawyer Group.

Gilles Valade

Gilles is presently an instructor with the School of Tourism at the University College of the Cariboo. He has a bachelor degree in Tourism Management (Adventure Tourism), a diploma in Adventure Tourism and a diploma in General Insurance. His involvement in the tourism industry includes guiding in eastern and western Canada, economic development and workshop design and delivery. Gilles also worked in the insurance industry for over 10 years as a commercial underwriter, a claims adjuster and the co-owner of an insurance-brokerage firm. He holds the Associate designation from the Insurance Institute of Canada.